A Kabbalah *of* Food

A Kabbalah of Food

Stories, Teachings, Recipes

Rabbi Hanoch Hecht

Monkfish Book Publishing Company
Rhinebeck, New York

Paperback ISBN: 978-1-948626-31-6
eBook ISBN: 978-1-948626-32-3

Library of Congress Cataloging-in-Publication Data
Names: Hecht, Hanoch, author.
Title: A kabbalah of food : stories, teachings, recipes / Rabbi Hanoch
    Hecht.
Description: Rhinebeck, NY : Monkfish Book Publishing Company, [2020] |
    Includes index.
Identifiers: LCCN 2020025996 (print) | LCCN 2020025997 (ebook) | ISBN
    9781948626316 (paperback) | ISBN 9781948626323 (ebook)
Subjects: LCSH: Hasidic parables. | Food--Religious aspects--Judaism. |
    Hasidim--Legends.
Classification: LCC BM532 .H37 2020 (print) | LCC BM532 (ebook) | DDC
    296.7/3--dc23
LC record available at https://lccn.loc.gov/2020025996
LC ebook record available at https://lccn.loc.gov/2020025997

Cover art: *Shabbat Table* © Michoel Muchnik
Seder plate illustration and author photo © Susan Piperato 2020
Book and cover design by Colin Rolfe

Monkfish Book Publishing Company
22 East Market Street, Suite 304
Rhinebeck, NY 12572
(845) 876-4861
monkfishpublishing.com

This book was written in the hope that these stories, teachings, and recipes bring readers closer to observing *kashrut* properly and to elevating the sparks of godliness within the physical world.

And to Gedalia Dovid and Devorah Shifra, who have taught me the meaning of giving without receiving anything in return.
May Hashem bless you with only open and revealed goodness.

Contents

Part 2: Recipes

CONTENTS

INTRODUCTION

NOTHING IS more central to Jewish life than food and storytelling. In fact, in Judaism, food is an integral part of religious practice, from observing the many laws of keeping kosher to the ritual preparation and eating of the special foods connected to the many Jewish holidays and Jewish culture.

I have always loved eating food—who doesn't?!—but the way I came to love cooking is another matter. When I was a *yeshiva* student, I was a bit of a wiseacre. I couldn't refrain from telling jokes in class, sometimes at the expense of my poor teachers. Consequently, they often asked me to leave the classroom. They assumed I would hang out in the hallways and get caught by the principal, who would then send me home so my parents would have the opportunity to deal with me. But since I didn't relish the thought of that, I would instead head to the cafeteria to see Mrs. Kraus, a wonderful elderly lady who was our school's cook. In return for my help with the chores, Mrs. Kraus would share some of the secrets of her preparations. Thus, I not only avoided the wrath of my parents, but I also learned early in life to love cooking and being in the kitchen.

When I was young, I also learned to love storytelling. In a Chassidic home, storytelling is a way of life. The stories come from our elders' own lives or the Hebrew Bible—or they are mystical, folktale-like accounts of events in the lives of the Chassidic masters and their followers. Through all these stories, children learn the Jewish principles and guidelines, and about morals. Of course, you can also teach children these things in other ways, but if you want to make a real impression, warm their hearts and create within them a love and caring for certain subjects, there's no better way than with a story. That's especially true if the stories are entertaining, heartfelt, humorous, or humbling—like the ones told in my home. For example, my grandfather, bless his memory, used to tell us a story about seeing his childhood friend again at his thirtieth-year high school reunion.

"So, what do you do for a living?" my grandfather's friend asked him.

"I'm a rabbi," my grandfather replied.

"Oh," his friend said, surprised. "But I thought you wanted to be an attorney."

My grandfather smiled, shaking his head. "I did," he said, "but then I realized it's easier to preach than it is to practice."

With that story, my grandfather was teaching us about the difference between practicing one's faith and talking about it. He also used to teach us about humility through stories like this one:

Once there was a young man who was the son of a rabbi and also became a rabbi himself. On the day of the young man's ordination, his father pulled him aside and told him, "Son, when you go to Heaven, you won't see any rabbis there, but when you go to hell, there you will see many."

That was, of course, a memorable way for my grandfather to show us that being a rabbi doesn't necessarily guarantee a person's holiness. Significantly, not only was my grandfather a rabbi, but so was my father, and so am I. Indeed, I come from a large family with many rabbis, both here in the United States and abroad.

In Hebrew, the word for "action" is *ma'a'seh*. As our rabbis say, *Ha 'Ma'a'seh, hu ha'ikar*: "Talk is cheap; action is what matters." Talking and preaching about giving charity is nice, but it means nothing. You've actually got to give charity. In Yiddish, the similar word *ma'sa'leh* means "story." There's a saying, *Ha 'Ma'sa'leh, hu ha'ikar*: "The story itself is the fundamental point." If you're trying to have a lasting effect on your listeners, inspiring them to action, then storytelling is the way.

THE WORD *kabbalah* means "to receive." It's a tradition that began with the giving of the Torah at Mount Sinai. At that awesome event, all the living men, women, and children of the Jewish faith were present, along with the souls of every future generation of Jews, and they received the Torah along with the Kabbalah, which is the Torah's mystical part. At first, only people of great spiritual and intellectual caliber could study Kabbalah, and only in secret; it was not until the sixteenth century that Rabbi Isaac Luria, known as the Arizal, "the lion," advocated for the masses to begin studying the Torah's mystical aspects. In fact, modern-day Kabbalah begins with the Arizal, who is a very interesting figure. As a young man, he spent many years living in a hut on a riverbank, delving into the secrets of the Torah and reading mystical books like the Zohar and the Sefer Yetzirah. In this way, he learned the magical aspect of Kabbalah and how to manipulate the physical world, and he used these secrets to strengthen Judaism and teach people to connect to God at a deeper level.

Initially, certain guidelines were followed for Kabbalah study. One needed to acquire a certain level of maturity as well as an understanding of many of the Torah's other teachings. It was thought that if someone studied the Kabbalah before being ready, he could come up with the wrong understanding of both God and life itself. The Talmud contains a story illustrating this point:

Once there were four rabbis who *entered the garden*, meaning they underwent a powerful Kabbalistic experience, and each one was affected differently by it. As soon as the first rabbi left the garden, he passed away. His soul couldn't handle such an intense mystical experience and left his body. His soul effectively said, "No more! I no longer want the physical world; I only want the glory of God."

The second rabbi's body could not handle what he encountered in the garden, and he emerged completely insane.

The third rabbi became a heretic: He lost his faith and denied the existence of God. The garden had changed his paradigm, or way of looking at things. Although he had always been a great scholar, he had not been mature enough to enter the garden.

But the fourth rabbi, Rabbi Akiva, was completely unchanged by the garden. He was a man of such great maturity and understanding that he was ready for a powerful mystical experience.

My students often ask, "What is the purpose of the Kabbalah?" One answer is: "What is the purpose of the Torah?" Since Kabbalah is part of the Torah, we need to engage the Torah in all its facets to understand Kabbalah. The purpose of the Torah, and hence Kabbalah, is wrapped up in the creation of the world, which is imperfect. Because of the world's imperfection, we are called and empowered to perfect ourselves and the world around us and to create a dwelling place for God's essence in this world. The Torah is a blueprint of the world being created historically and recreated constantly, from moment to moment, and it's a guide for how we humans should live.

The Chassidic movement has made the study of Kabbalah and the mystical part of the Torah central to daily life. This way of life is deeply tied to Rabbi Israel ben Eliezer, known as the Ba'al Shem Tov, "master of the good name of God" (1698–1760). After losing his parents when he was five years old, the Ba'al Shem Tov was raised by his uncle. Perhaps because he didn't receive the love in his uncle's house that he would have gotten from his parents, he spent a lot of time by himself in the nearby fields and forests when he was very young.

As a teenager, he became curious about the world and began wandering farther and farther away on his own. One day he met a group of mystics who traveled from town to town, and from then on, he spent time with them whenever they came through his village; eventually, he joined their society. At the age of twenty-six, the Ba'al Shem Tov began studying with Achiya Hashiloni, a mystical figure who had taught Elijah the prophet some 1,500 years before. How this happened remains a mystery. Did Achiya Hashiloni come in the physical body from the spiritual world to teach the Ba'al Shem Tov, or was the Ba'al Shem Tov able to travel to the spiritual world? We don't know, but whichever way you look at it, each figure is a phenomenon.

At the age of thirty-six, Achiya Hashiloni told the Ba'al Shem Tov, "Now is your moment to begin revealing yourself to the masses and start teaching." The Ba'al Shem Tov refused, so Achiya Hashiloni told him, "This is your purpose in the world, and if you won't do it, there's no reason for us to continue studying together." It was only after losing his connection to Achiya Hashiloni that the Ba'al Shem Tov began to reveal himself. Going from town to town, the Ba'al Shem Tov shared many innovations in Judaism. He taught that the act of loving thy neighbor is a way of reenergizing and reawakening of the Jewish spirit, emphasized the importance of sincerity over scholarship, and showed how even simple and unlearned Jews also have value and the ability to connect to God. Now was the time, he told his followers, for Kabbalah to be studied by the masses, as the Arizal had preached. In the Arizal's lifetime there had been some advancement in accessibility to Kabbalah, but there were still limitations. The Ba'al Shem Tov favored ending those limitations. He wanted everyone to study Kabbalah and learn the secrets of the Torah.

The Ba'al Shem Tov innovated even further by founding the study of *Chassidut*. As to the distinction between the two, "Kabbalah," writes Rabbi Adin Steinsaltz, "is the study of Torah's inner meaning and the structure of the spiritual universe and its relationship to our own world. Chassidut, in contrast, is the exploration of how we can apply Kabbalah to our own lives."

Unfortunately, some people view Chassidut as watered-down Kabbalah, but Chassidut actually takes the study of the secrets of the Torah to a new level. Often, where Kabbalah seems to contradict the literal understanding of the Torah, Chassidut can sew a thread between the different levels of understanding, showing how it is all one. (That's why, in this book, I use the terms Chassidut and Kabbalah somewhat interchangeably.)

The Ba'al Shem Tov believed studying Chassidut was relevant for every single person; to him, even a child learning the verses of the Torah should be taught some of its mystical secrets. In the Chassidic tradition, when we teach a child the Hebrew alphabet, or *aleph-bet*, we begin with the first letter, the *aleph*, which consists of a line and two dots, a *vov* and two *yud*. The child wonders, why is this letter shaped this way; what does it represent? We explain that the yud above the line represents God, and yud below the line stands for man, while the line in between symbolizes our connection to God. In this way, we begin to introduce Kabbalistic concepts to children as young as three or four years old as they learn to read and write.

The Ba'al Shem Tov amassed many students, and those who reached a certain level of understanding and maturity joined what was called the *Chevraya Kadisha*, the Holy Society. The last student to join was Dov Ber of Mezeritch, also known as the Maggid of Mezeritch, who became the Ba'al Shem Tov's successor as leader of the Chassidic movement. Shortly thereafter, Chassidism spread at such a rate that Chassidic masters were given territories to oversee. In White Russia, Rabbi Shneur Zalman of Liadi, affectionately known as the Alter Rebbe, began taking an intellectual approach to the teachings of the Maggid and the Ba'al Shem Tov and founded *Chabad Chassidut.*

Shneur Zalman's approach was very controversial, and many Chassidic masters did not agree with him. The *Chassidic Chagas*, for instance, believed that a rebbe functioned as a kind of train conductor, and a student's only requirement was to get aboard, whereas the Alter Rebbe felt that every person was his own driver. He created a vigorous study program for his followers, including study groups for various levels of understanding. The Chabad movement continues in a similar fashion today.

———— ◦◦◦ ————

JUDAISM IS unique among religions for having many laws connected to food. Other religions have rules forbidding followers from eating certain foods, but Judaism includes not only prohibitions, but also strict laws regarding what is kosher and therefore edible. Such laws are called *kashrut,* and they tell us what foods can be consumed together, when certain foods should be eaten, and how all our food must be prepared. Each food group—meat, fish, milk, eggs, poultry, produce—has many complex laws associated with it. For instance, when it comes to meat, a kosher animal must be identified as such, and its life must be taken instantaneously, without causing any pain, using certain utensils. Once the animal's life is taken, its blood as well as certain fats must be removed through a soaking and salting process.

There are also many laws regarding how we eat. According to the Talmud, putting a piece of food into our mouth without saying a blessing is stealing from Heaven. After we finish eating, we must make another blessing, thanking God for giving us the food. And finally, once we have finished eating, we must transform the food's energy into something positive—taking the physical and turning it into the spiritual. Just as food provides physical energy, so too it gives us the energy to perform *mitzvot*—acts of spirituality.

This emphasis on food is extended to all of the Jewish holidays. Each holiday has its own laws associated with food: what we can't eat and what we can or should eat. On Passover, you can't eat leavened bread, so you eat matzah; on Rosh Hashanah, you eat symbolic foods. On Sukkot, you have to eat in a *sukkah*, a hut outside your home, built just for the holiday.

One of the fundamental parts of studying to become a rabbi is learning the many laws of kosher; when I was studying, we joked that the only reason anyone studies kashrut is to learn how much they don't know!

How many stories in the Torah are associated with food? So many! For instance, there are stories about the Jewish people complaining about not having meat, manna coming from Heaven, Abraham telling his son to go get food for himself and his guest, and Lot and the salt— to name a few. Why so many stories about food? Judaism has survived for close to 3,300 years not because of the Temple, which was twice destroyed, but because of the Jewish home; for Jews, food has a strong social aspect. Sometimes, people who come to *shul* after a long time away tell me, "Rabbi, this is a great place, but I'm never coming back." But if I offer them a homemade potato knish, they want to come back! It's not because of the way the potato knish tastes, which is great; it's because there's an inherent spiritual connection made.

By eating that knish, a person's soul understands that its job in the physical world is to take physicality, in the form of a potato knish, and turn it into spirituality. The soul understands that the body's purpose is to be a dwelling place for God in this world, and that is most easily accomplished through eating. Food is a central part of our connection to God and how we perform mitzvot. That's why people say that when a Jew walks into a shul, the herring—or the potato knish—talks to him.

The word kosher means "fit," as in "fit to eat." Many people assume that kashrut is strictly concerned with healthy eating, but that's not the case. It's true that a kosher piece of chicken goes through a salting process that removes bacteria—and through the ages, such kosher preparations have been documented to protect the Jewish people from widespread diseases—but kosher doesn't mean healthier or cleaner.

Nor is kosher necessarily concerned with ethics. For instance, there are no kosher laws regarding whether or not an employee involved in a food's preparation was paid minimum wage, though those types of issues are also discussed in the Torah. Instead, kosher tells us how to behave toward food in the way Torah lays out. For instance, if someone eats kosher food quickly, mindlessly, like an animal—then thank God it's kosher, so at least he didn't sin. But according to Chassidut, by eating fast and mindlessly that person isn't spiritually elevating the food either.

There's a Chassidic saying: "That which is forbidden, we surely can't have. That which we can have, we don't always need." In other words, just because something is permitted by law doesn't mean we should go ahead and have a lot of it. I love ice cream, and ice cream is permitted, but that doesn't mean I should eat it every day. Just because you keep kosher doesn't mean you're allowed to eat something thoughtlessly. Kosher foods must be eaten in the proper way. Keeping kosher is a bit like playing baseball. Each time we sit down to eat, it's like getting up to bat. Will we hit or strike out? In other words, are we using the food and the act of eating to connect to God, or simply satisfying our physical hunger?

There's a story about Shmuel Munkes, a famous follower of the Rebbe Shneur Zalman of Liadi. He was quite a prankster, but his actions always carried great meaning. One day he traveled to visit his friend named Peretz, who was also a great *Chassid*. Peretz said, "Shmuel, my house is open to you, so make yourself at home. Whatever you want here is yours." So when Shmuel woke up at three o'clock in the morning, he went down to the kitchen and made coffee. He thought, "Since Peretz knows I'm here, he'll wake up early to spend time with me, and we can study together." And he sat drinking his coffee, and everything was good.

Sure enough, Peretz woke up soon afterward, went to the kitchen, washed his hands, said his morning blessings, and turned to Shmuel and said, "Thank you so much for making me a cup of coffee." Smiling, he picked up his coffee cup, took a sip—and spat it right out.

"What's wrong with you?!" he shouted.

"What do you mean?" Shmuel replied. "I made coffee for you!"

"This coffee!" Peretz sputtered. "Where did you take it from?"

"From the cabinet," Shmuel said.

Peretz ran to the cabinet, flung it open, and looked inside. "That's not coffee, that's snuff!" he shouted. "Shmuel, how are you drinking this?!"

Shmuel shrugged. "I didn't realize it wasn't coffee," he said. "I trained myself at my first private audience with the Rebbe not to take pleasure from the physical world."

Will following the laws of kosher change you? Definitely! Kosher makes you more aware. That's the whole point of kosher. You'll begin asking yourself, "Am I going to make a blessing?" When you see a piece of chicken on your plate, you'll understand what was sacrificed in order for you to go through the process of eating and spiritually elevating it. Although I don't embrace the philosophy of veganism, I believe its purpose is similar to kosher's: to wake people up. With kosher, that's true not just about animals but about all foods. God constantly recreates the world every second. Every tomato, every leaf of lettuce contains a spark of godliness. Even though that piece of lettuce didn't go around clucking like a chicken before it was plucked and put into your salad, it nevertheless contains a spark of godliness, and it too had a life, so you have to eat it in a way that elevates it spiritually. The question is not, "If I eat kosher, will I feel it?" No! But every time you sit down to eat, you'll appreciate the food and eat it with proper intention, making sure its godly spark is acknowledged and elevated.

For some people, like Shmuel Munkes, the way to God is by removing themselves. For other people, pure enjoyment is the way, and this book is full of stories about that. God put physical pleasure into the world, so by indulging correctly, we can connect to God on a deeper level. So, what's the difference between pleasure for me and pleasure in God? I can eat a plate of food and experience pleasure for myself by feeding my animalistic soul, my ego. Or I can eat for God, experiencing the same amount of pleasure but understanding that it was God who put these foods in the world for me to enjoy. The blessings we say before we eat food are called the Blessings of Enjoyment for this reason. Does God participate in our pleasure? Absolutely! He wants us to experience the pleasure of the physical world, but He wants us to do it in a way that is holy.

Isaac, the second of our forefathers, had twin sons: Jacob, who chose the path of spirituality and godliness, and Esau, who chose the path of the unholy. When Isaac was 123 years old, blind, and on his deathbed, he called in Esau and offered to give him a blessing. But the way he put it was interesting: "I want to bless you before I die, but first, bring me a meal of delicacies and delicious foods that I love."

So Esau went off to find his father a fine meal, but unbeknownst to him, his mother, Rebecca, had overheard Isaac's offering. Rebecca's favorite son was Jacob, because she knew he was the best of the two, so she called Jacob to her and told him, "Your father has offered to bless your brother, but you have to go in and get the blessing. I am going to cook your father's favorite dinner for you to bring to him."

Now, this story introduces one of the greatest Kabbalistic concepts: Why did Jacob have to steal the blessing? Because this world is upside down, and in an upside-down world, in order to elevate it, sometimes you have to use forms of trickery. The true existence is spiritual. We see what is physical. How do we unleash the spiritual? Sometimes we have to use forms of deception to bring about that which is spiritually proper. Yes, Jacob stole the blessing, but really it was his blessing. Esau had sold Jacob the blessing twenty-four years earlier. So essentially Jacob's stance was, "Hey, Dad, I know you want to bless Esau, but look, here's the contract. He sold it to me. The blessing rightfully comes to me."

But let's get back to the food in this story. Rebecca cooked a delicious meal, and Jacob brought it to Isaac and was given the highest of all blessings by him.

When I first heard this story as a child, I wondered, what has food got to do with the spiritual act of blessing? A father places his hands on his son's head and says, "God should bless you. He should give you livelihood. He should give you sustenance. He should give you all the good things. You shouldn't have to struggle in this life." Then the father gives his son a kiss and sends him off into the world. Giving a blessing is usually very straightforward, but not so in this story. Isaac had to have his favorite foods first. Why? Because enjoying that meal allowed him to reach the greater dimension of spirituality required for him to give his son that blessing.

As I grew up, I came to understand and embrace the concepts presented by the story of Isaac blessing Jacob, and to appreciate how deeply this story resonates with the central theme of food that runs through Judaism. Cooking, sharing, and enjoying food, as demonstrated by this collection of Chassidic tales, creates a dwelling place for God within us and allows us to elevate the spark of godliness within the physical world. If we prepare our food properly and eat and share it mindfully and joyfully, then each and every morsel can reveal to us the spiritual dimension within everything.

—*Rabbi Hanoch Hecht*

PART 1

Stories

and

Teachings

THE MYSTERY OF KABBALAH

The Mystical Cakes

O NCE, ABOUT five hundred years ago, in old Europe, a very wealthy gentleman married his daughter off to a smart and talented young man. The gentleman gave the young couple a huge dowry, wishing them the greatest happiness together. However, within the first few weeks of marriage, tragedy struck, and the bride passed away. In the midst of mourning the death of his daughter, the gentleman decided to go and see his son-in-law about some business: He wanted the dowry back.

"The only reason I gave you this money was because you were marrying my daughter and you were going to have a life together," he told his son-in-law. "You're a nice guy and all, but now that my daughter is gone, there's no reason for you to keep this money of mine."

His son-in-law disagreed with him, and their dispute heated up. Finally, they agreed to have their argument vetted, so they went to see the Arizal, Rabbi Isaac Luria.

Together, the gentleman and his son-in-law stood before the Arizal, who told them, "I'll listen to your case, but only on one condition: Whatever decision I make will be final, and I don't have to give you any reason for my decision." The two men agreed and presented their sides of the case to the Arizal, who sided 100 percent with the son-in-law.

"Why?" demanded the angry gentleman, immediately forgetting that the Arizal's decision was to be final. "How could you make this decision? What's your *halachic* reasoning?"

The Arizal refused to give any ground. "I told you the condition for my hearing your case was that you are not allowed to question my decision," he reminded the father-in-law, "so I'm not going to answer you."

The gentleman was not only angry, but also very hurt, and he went around speaking not so nicely about the Arizal to everyone he met. Finally, he consulted Reb Maharshal Moreinu Shlomo Luria, who was one of the greatest Polish Talmudists. When the rabbi heard the gentleman's story, he decided to write the Arizal a very harsh letter criticizing his decision.

Now, the Arizal was in the practice of taking a few of his prized students and teaching them, through Kabbalah, how to travel very long distances in a very short time. (Back then, the magical part of Kabbalah was still being practiced.) When the Arizal received the letter from Reb Maharshal Moreinu Shlomo Luria, he told his students, "When you go home tonight, have your wives bake some fresh cakes. When the cakes are steaming hot, right out of the oven, take them and immediately travel all the way across Europe to Reb Maharshal Moreinu Shlomo Luria's study hall. When you get there I want you to walk into the Rebbe's studio, holding the cakes up high so that everyone can see that the cakes are steaming, because they will still be hot.

"Of course," the Arizal continued, "they'll ask you, 'Why are you holding forth those cakes?' You'll tell them, 'Our wives just baked them.' Then they'll ask you, 'Where do you live?' And you'll tell them, 'We live across the globe.' You must meet with Rebbe Yechiel Emden and defend my honor. This is the story I want you to tell him:

"There were once two men who were the best of friends, so they decided to go into business together. They did very well, and everything was going fine until greed got the best of one partner and he decided to rob his best friend of all the money they had made. His friend soon became so poor that he actually died from starvation.

"Eventually, the rich man also passed away and went up to Heaven. When he reached Heaven, he was told that since it was his fault that his partner had died, he was going straight to purgatory. The only problem was that the rich man's former partner, who had died of poverty and hunger as the result of having been cheated, still loved him—and even still considered the rich man his best friend. 'No, please,' the wronged partner said, 'I don't want my friend to go to purgatory.'

"This incited a big argument in Heaven. Some said that, based on the rich man's thievery, he should go to hell, and yet the very person who had been wronged by him was advocating for him to remain in Heaven, and not even go to purgatory. Finally, it was decided that the two former partners and best friends should come back into this world so that the partner who did the wrong could give the money back to the rightful owner."

The Arizal explained that the gentleman was the reincarnation of the thieving partner. and his son-in-law was the reincarnation of the partner who had been robbed and died of starvation. Now, in this lifetime, the wronged partner had received the money back. "And so," the Arizal concluded, "we have to take into consideration other factors beyond that which we can see with the naked eye."

TEACHING

Coming to a full understanding of the story of "The Mystical Cakes," requires having some background knowledge. Traditionally, according to Jewish law, a husband takes possession of his wife's property immediately upon marriage. But because the chances of dying young were high in Old Europe due to pogroms as well as epidemics such as the plague, the Ashkenazi (Eastern European) Jews passed an edict stating that if a wife passed away within the first year of marriage, her husband had to return her dowry to her parents, his in-laws. The Sephardic Jews (descended from the Iberian Peninsula), however, continued to follow the traditional Jewish law.

In this story, the young couple is Ashkenazi, so technically, the bereaved son-in-law should have had to return the dowry to his bride's father. That's why the bride's father consulted the Arizal, Rabbi Isaac Luria (1532-1572), who essentially said, "You're Ashkenazi, and therefore you have to follow the edict proclaiming that a husband doesn't inherit his wife's dowry until after the first twelve months of marriage." So, it was no wonder that the father-in-law became very angry and went around Europe complaining about the Arizal taking the Sephardic point of view.

But perhaps even more important is coming to an understanding of the most dramatic part of the story: the Arizal's followers flying halfway across the world with cakes still warm from the oven to show that Maharshal Moreinu

Shlomo Luria was wrong. Why such a dramatic act, and how did the group of followers accomplish such a miracle?

The Kabbalah has three aspects: theoretical, meditative, and magical. The Arizal was a master of magical Kabbalah. As a young man, he lived for many years in a hut by a river, spending his days delving into the secrets of the Torah and the mystical part of Judaism. He also studied books like the Sefer Yetzirah, which focuses on the earliest Kabbalistic texts and describes the secrets and powers involved in the creation of the world. In this way, the Arizal learned to surpass some of the normal limitations that humans experience in the physical world. Many of the stories that have been passed down about the Arizal (and the Ba'al Shem Tov) involve the use of such magical powers, including traveling great distances in a short period of time and seeing into a person's past and future incarnations. The Arizal used the magical aspect of Kabbalah for good, to strengthen Judaism and teach people to connect to a deeper level, a mystical level, to God.

Theoretical Kabbalah, which is largely based on the Zohar, is concerned with the structure and dynamics of the spiritual worlds, the Sefirot, souls, and angels.

Through the meditative aspect of the Kabbalah, we learn about the makeup of the soul and the spiritual worlds and how God created and interacts with the world. This study can lead us to a very deep level of mediation, so that when we pray, perform mitzvot, or study Torah we are able to do so more deeply. Most importantly, it teaches us how to connect with God and fulfill the special destiny for which we were born. Meditative Kabbalah also deals with methods to reach higher states of consciousness, such as the use of divine names and permutations of the Hebrew letters. Most of the main texts on meditative Kabbalah have never been published and remain scattered in manuscripts in libraries and museums around the world.

While meditative and theoretical Kabbalah have experienced a resurgence with the rise of the Chassidic movement, magical Kabbalah is no longer studied or practiced. The Talmud includes a story explaining why:

Once there were two rabbis who were very good friends, and one year they decided to celebrate the holiday of Purim together. They became so spiritually intoxicated that they were able to travel through the spiritual realms, with one rabbi guiding the other. But for the second rabbi, the experience was so intense that he lost his conscious self, and his soul left his body. It was as if he had been struck dead, murdered. The rabbi who was leading the way had to restore the second rabbi's soul to his body.

A year later, the first rabbi asked the second rabbi to celebrate Purim with him again. But the second rabbi, whose soul had to be brought back to his body, declined. "No, thank you," he told his friend. "Last year was too intense." The experience had upset his entire sense of being, and it was as if he had been resurrected from the dead.

The seventh Lubavitcher Rebbe, Menachem Mendel Schneerson (1902-1994), once gave a great talk about this story. The Rebbe asked, "What is the second rabbi so worried about? If they get so spiritually drunk that he gets murdered again, what's the big deal? He'll be brought back to life." The lesson is that the experience, which involved the magical aspect of the Kabbalah, was so frightening that it should not repeated. The first rabbi had taken the second rabbi on such an intense experience that the second rabbi lost his conscious self, and essentially had to be resurrected from the dead. You can't expect your soul to experience an awesome Kabbalistic event and then simply come back into your body. It might not happen.

The Mysterious City

ONE OF the Ba'al Shem Tov's *Chassidim* was in the business of buying and selling goods, but he realized that since he just wasn't getting ahead, he needed to try a new approach. So he and his wife decided that he should travel to another country, buy goods at a better price, and bring them back home to sell; that way, they thought, they could begin to make a real profit.

Before leaving for his trip, the Chassid went to see his rebbe, the Ba'al Shem Tov, who blessed him for a safe journey. The ship set sail on smooth waters, but suddenly, in the middle of the very first night at sea, a storm hit. Soon the ship was rocking back and forth, back and forth, with waves crashing over its sides. The passengers joined the crew to try to bail the ship out, but eventually, the ship could no longer handle all the water it had taken on, and it began to sink. Everybody grabbed onto whatever they could to stay afloat. When the ship went down, the Chassid was holding onto a plank for dear life, and he was knocked unconscious.

When he awakened, he found himself washed up on an island, all alone. He began walking, searching for other people—but he could not find anyone, so he kept walking, on and on. Finally, as the sun was setting and he reached the other end of the island, the Chassid saw a city in the distance. He ran toward it eagerly, hoping to find someone who could tell him where he was.

But the city was completely silent, and even though the Chassid knocked on the doors of one house after another, no one answered. Although the city appeared as if people were living there—with shops and synagogues and office buildings and street lamps and houses with charming little gardens and curtained windows—the Chassid discovered that all the buildings were actually empty. Strangely, there wasn't a soul around.

After a long time of knocking, the Chassid realized that since it was late, he should enter one of the houses, so he chose one with a *mezuzah* over the front door. The door, he was surprised to discover, was not even locked, and even though nobody was inside the house, he found food. Amazingly, the food was even kosher, and the Chassid helped himself to something to eat. He could tell it was a Torah-observant home that followed all of the commandments and mitzvot, but he didn't know quite what to make of it all. On top of that, he was very tired, so he found a bedroom and went to sleep.

When he awoke the next morning, the city was still silent. The Chassid went back to the kitchen and found even more kosher food— gefilte fish, herring, challah—and ate another meal. Then he wandered around the empty city some more, knocking on doors, but still he found no human beings.

Each day was the same: the Chassid found food stored in the kitchen to eat, spent the day walking the city alone, and went home to eat and go to sleep. Then, one morning, he awoke to sounds outside. He ran to the front door and threw it open to find that the city was filled with life. He couldn't believe the hustle and bustle before his eyes! People were rushing to and from the marketplace, carrying home bottles of wine and parcels of fish, meat, and challah. They were also hurrying in and out of the doors of the nearby *mikveh*—and in the windows of the houses across the street, the Chassid could see women setting their tables, getting the candles ready to light, and performing all manner of preparations for the holy Shabbat day.

The Chassid, who was overjoyed not to be alone anymore yet still felt perplexed, managed to grab a man as he rushed past. "Tell me, sir, what's going on here!" he demanded. "Where did you come from?"

"You've got to ask the rabbi," the man said.

"Where does the rabbi live?"

"In that house over there."

The Chassid walked over to the rabbi's house and knocked on the door. "Rabbi!" he cried when the rabbi welcomed him inside. "You have to tell me what's going on! Where am I? Why was this city empty until this morning? Where did all these people suddenly come from?"

"Why don't you get ready for Shabbat and join us tonight?" the rabbi answered calmly. "Then I shall explain."

"Sure, that sounds wonderful," the Chassid replied. He ran back to the house where he had left his belongings, and hastily got ready. He accompanied the rabbi to shul and marveled at the joyful service. People were chanting, singing songs, and dancing—it was all like something from another world, and the Chassid was in ecstasy. Afterwards, he went home with the rabbi and sat down to enjoy a delicious meal with all the Shabbat delicacies. At the end of the meal, he said, "Rabbi, please tell me, what's going on here?"

The rabbi smiled and shook his head. "Listen, it's late now," he said. "Let's go to sleep. Tomorrow is a big day."

The Chassid retired to the rabbi's guest room, and fell into the deepest sleep. The next morning, he accompanied the rabbi back to the synagogue for another beautiful service, then went home with him for another delicious meal. Everything was fantastic, perfect, off the charts. "Tell me, please, what's going on?" he begged the rabbi. "I have to know."

But the rabbi said, "Now it's time for a Shabbat nap. Let's talk later."

Again, the Chassid retired to the guest room, where he once more fell into the deepest sleep and woke up an hour later feeling refreshed and rejuvenated.

"Please, what's going on here?" he implored the rabbi.

But the rabbi simply smiled and shook his head once again. "Now we have to go to shul for afternoon services," he said.

Off they went to the afternoon services, and they stayed to pray at the evening services too. At last they walked home together. "Rabbi, please," the Chassid begged along the way, "you have to tell me what's going on. I can't stand this any longer."

"Let's make the *Havdalah*," the rabbi said. "Let's perform the ceremony in which we separate the holy Shabbat day from the rest of the week. Afterwards we'll talk."

So the rabbi made the Havdalah, the closing ceremony after Shabbat, and as he did, he and everyone else in the city vanished in a flash. The

Chassid was the only soul left in the entire place. He didn't know what to do. Once again, he ran from house to house, knocking on doors, but he heard nothing and found no one. He couldn't fathom what was going on. Finally, he was so exhausted that he returned to the rabbi's house. Back in the rabbi's guest room, he fell once again into the deepest sleep.

Another week passed in the same way as before. The Chassid stayed at the rabbi's house, ate Shabbat leftovers, walked through the silent but lovely city each day, and then returned home to sleep more deeply than he had ever thought possible. Although he was constantly on the lookout for the return of the rabbi and the rest of the city's population, he saw no one and heard nothing.

But then, once again, on Friday morning, he was awakened by a hustle and a bustle outside, and when he got up to throw open the front door, there stood the rabbi. The sequence of events from the previous weekend repeated itself, with the Chassid remaining a guest in the rabbi's house. But as the end of Shabbat approached, the Chassid became completely frantic to understand what was happening.

"Rabbi," he shouted on the way home from the synagogue, nearly in tears, "you've got to tell me, what is going on?"

"Wait for Havdalah," the rabbi answered.

This time the Chassid had a plan. Before the rabbi finished the Havdalah prayer, the Chassid grabbed his arm and held on tight. "I'm not letting you go anywhere," he told the rabbi, "until you explain to me what's going on."

The rabbi sighed. "All right," he said. "I don't want to tell anyone our secret, but since you've merited to see all this, obviously, you deserve to know. We are a community that dates back to the time of the destruction of the Second Temple. During our lives, we all had a tremendous love for the holy Shabbat day. We demonstrated such care, such dedication, and such self-sacrifice during our lives that, when we went up to Heaven, we were allowed to return to this secret city back on earth every single Friday to experience Shabbat in the physical world. That is why every Friday we come, and also why, after Havdalah, we all go back to our place in eternity.

"I can offer you two options," the rabbi continued. "You can join us for eternity on our journey. We go to the other world during the week, and we come back to the physical world for Shabbat. Or, if you prefer, I can send you back to your family."

The man thought it over for a while. Finally, he said, "As much as I'd like to join you, I don't think it would be fair to my wife and children. Therefore, I'm going to ask you to send me back to my family."

The rabbi nodded, his eyes full of feeling. "I understand," he said. He took out a quill and a piece of parchment on which he wrote the ineffable name of God. Then he folded up the parchment and told the man, "Hold onto this piece of paper, close your eyes, and imagine yourself going home. When you open your eyes, you'll be back in your village. When you reach your home, before you go inside throw this piece of paper up to Heaven. You'll see a hand reach down from the sky to catch it. And then your life will go back to normal."

The man took the piece of paper and, holding onto it tightly, he imagined sailing on a ship back home and then traveling in a carriage until he came to his village. When he opened his eyes, there he was, back in his village, standing before his house. As he walked toward his front door, he was about to throw the piece of paper up to Heaven when suddenly someone tapped him on the shoulder. He turned to see standing behind him none other than the Ba'al Shem Tov, who took the piece of paper from him. "I'm sure they won't miss this in Heaven," he said as he tucked the paper into his pocket. "I can use it to help a lot of people down on earth."

And the Ba'al Shem Tov turned and went on his way.

 TEACHING

When we experience Shabbat, we are blessed and bestowed with a *neshama y'eserah*, an extra soul, for the holy Shabbat day. This extra soul is not like having someone else's soul inside of ourselves—that would make us schizophrenic. Rather, having an additional soul gives us the capability of connecting to God and utilizing a higher level of our own soul. This extra soul allows us to indulge and delight in the spiritual as well as the physical, and to do so in a way that isn't normally possible during the week. Therefore, our entire week should be in preparation for the Shabbat so that when it arrives we are able to experience it and delight in it to the highest of levels.

According to Kabbalah, there are five levels of the soul; from the lowest to the highest level, they are *Nefesh, Ruach, Neshamah, Chaya,* and *Yechidah.* During the week, we are perhaps in touch with the two lowest levels of our souls: Nefesh and Ruach. But on Shabbat, the holy day of rest, a day of spirituality and godliness, we get in touch with the higher levels of the soul as well: Neshamah, and perhaps even Chaya and Yechidah.

The Four Sons, the Feast, and the Godly Spark

R EB YECHIEL Ashkenazi of Tolchyn was the son of a very wealthy man, and when he and his three brothers came of age, their father gave each one of them a sack of money. "Go out and find a path in your service to God," their father told them all. "In ten years, on Rosh Chodesh Tamuz [the first day of the month of Tamuz, which occurs during the American summer] in a certain city, we will meet again at a family reunion."

Of course, the brothers all lived long before the invention of social media, so they could not stay in touch at every moment; they all had to go out into the world truly on their own to find their paths of service to God. Along the way, Reb Yechiel met the Ba'al Shem Tov and received his teachings. He was such an outstanding student that the Ba'al Shem Tov invited him to join the Chevraya Kadisha, a holy society of prized, elite students which eventually grew to sixty members. The Ba'al Shem Tov valued Reb Yechiel so much that he even granted him permission to marry his only daughter, Udel.

Ten years slipped by quickly, and before Reb Yechiel knew it, it was time to reunite with his family. As soon as he arrived, he embraced his father and his brothers happily, feeling overjoyed to be with them again. In celebration of the family reunion and the brothers' scholarship, Reb Yechiel's father threw a *s'udas mitzvah*—a huge, festive meal—and invited the entire city to join in.

At the feast, the eldest son got up and gave a *pilpul*, a deep and detailed discourse on the Talmud, amazing the crowd with his scholarship. Then the second son followed with another pilpul, this time on

Jewish law, even tying in his older brother's discussion of the Talmud, and the crowd was so impressed that everyone agreed they hadn't witnessed scholarship like that in years and years.

Next, it was Reb Yechiel's turn to speak, but when his father invited him to stand up, he remained seated, eating the chicken and brisket and potato kugel and other delicious foods. Meanwhile, people kept approaching him, asking, "Wouldn't you like to talk and share your knowledge?" But Reb Yechiel took his time. Finally, he paused from eating, got up, and walked slowly over to the podium to give his speech. "I'd just like to announce that the food tonight is spectacular," he said. "You guys hired the best caterer! The food is delicious, especially the brisket." With that, he returned to his table, sat back down, picked up his fork, and continued eating.

Nobody in the crowd knew what to make of this behavior, so they all sat there, stunned, asking each other, "What's wrong with Reb Yechiel?" Fortunately, though, they were soon distracted by the fourth son, who gave another captivating pilpul.

At the end of the evening, when the celebration died down, the crowd was talking about two things: the wonderful scholarship of three of the four brothers and how Reb Yechiel had surprisingly grown up to be an odd, abrasive man and a bit of a *gornisht*—a nothing, an empty vessel.

That evening, back at the hotel, Reb Yechiel's father went to his son's room to speak to him about what had happened. "My dear son," his father began. "I thank God for having given me a tremendous amount of *nachas*—joy—through my children tonight. Your brothers showed that they truly have gained great knowledge of Torah and Judaism. But in you, unfortunately, I'm frankly very disappointed. You had at least as great if not greater talents and wisdom and comprehension as your brothers, yet you seem to have turned out to be a total failure and an embarrassment!"

Reb Yechiel, who loved his father very much, turned to him and said, "Father, I'm so sorry you feel this way, but why don't you throw another party tomorrow night? I'll speak then, and I promise not to disappoint you."

Reb Yechiel's father was overjoyed. He immediately called the caterers to return, and told them to have their workers spend the whole night and the next day preparing food for another grand party the next evening. Then the father set about inviting the entire city to the second party. Based on the delicacies they had enjoyed at the first party and the revelations of Torah and scholarship they had heard, nobody saw any reason at all why they should stay home this time. So all the guests not only returned, but brought with them even more family and friends, so this time, the crowd was even greater.

Once again, the first son got up and began giving a very wise Talmudic discourse. But in the middle of the speech, Reb Yechiel suddenly stood up, walked over to his brother, and touched his hand to his brother's forehead. Immediately, his brother's voice changed tone, and he began confessing every single sin he had ever committed in his life. With that, Reb Yechiel simply returned to his seat.

No one in the crowd knew what to make of this, but they were soon distracted by the second son, who went to the podium and began talking about Jewish Law. But once again, Reb Yechiel suddenly stood up again and walked over to his brother as he stood there speaking. Just as before, he touched the second brother's forehead, and this brother's voice changed too, and he began describing all of the sins he had ever committed.

Now it was Reb Yechiel's turn, and he stepped forward to the podium.

"My brothers and I were very blessed ten years ago when our father sent us all out to find a service and a path to God and a way to approach Torah and mitzvot—commandments and acts of goodness and kindness," Reb Yechiel told the crowd. "Thank God, along the way, I was introduced to the Ba'al Shem Tov and his teachings." He began discussing the Ba'al Shem Tov's innovative fundamental teachings, which were transforming the way people practiced Judaism. One of the Ba'al Shem Tov's most important innovations was the embracing of the physical, Reb Yechiel told the crowd. "Man is comprised of body and soul, and his soul has to direct his physical body to take that which is physical and material and turn it into spirituality and holiness," he said. "That is man's job on earth.

"But last night," Reb Yechiel continued, "everybody was so focused on spirituality and scholarship that they forgot to pay proper respect to the material in this room—the wonderful food—and they neglected to focus on elevating the godly spark within our dinner. So when I complimented the food, it wasn't that I'm just a gluttonous individual focused on food—on eating the delicious brisket. Rather, I was focusing on the physical and the need to elevate the spark of godliness within the food by connecting it to its source."

 TEACHING

This story is important historically because it recounts how Reb Yechiel was able to introduce the teachings of the Ba'al Shem Tov to people in another part of the world who were not familiar with them. According to Chassidic history, the revelation of the Ba'al Shem Tov took place during a period in which Judaism was being repressed, shortly after the pogrom that preceded the appearance of Shabtai Tzvi, the false messiah. At that time, being a good Jew was measured by how much knowledge one had amassed and how ascetic one was, and Judaism was devoid of happiness and joy. But the Ba'al Shem Tov's mission was to reinvigorate and reawaken the Jewish spirit. It was no coincidence that he was called Israel, the name of the Jewish people.

Despite the Ba'al Shem Tov's innovations being challenged, he gave his sixty elite students, including Reb Yechiel Ashkenazi, the directive to spread his teachings throughout the Jewish world. Reb Yechiel not only saw elevating the physical, especially food, as his own mission, but he also saw food as a way to make people aware of the Ba'al Shem Tov and his teachings.

This story has many important aspects. First, it brings into play the fundamental principles and teachings of Kabbalah and the Chassidic direction of behavior, which is all about acting with humility. Why did Reb Yechiel embarrass his brothers? Because each of his brothers stood up at the celebration and spoke boastfully, lacking the humility that one needs to have when approaching the study of Torah. In other words, they showed off. We all have to strive to work on ourselves. Ego can be at the root of many negative character traits, and we must try to rid ourselves of it. Healthy humility is a major element of the teachings of the Ba'al Shem Tov.

The Tzaddik's Evil Spirits

ONCE, WHEN an innkeeper and his family were thrown into debtors' prison by the local land squire, the *poritz,* for not paying their rent, the Ba'al Shem Tov decided to perform the great mitzvah of *Pidyon Sh'vuyim,* redeeming captives. First, he went around to everyone in the town, fundraising for the innkeeper. When he had raised enough money to pay the innkeeper's back rent, he gathered together a few of his *talmidim*—the student members of his holy society of mystics—and took them with him to see the squire. As soon as the Ba'al Shem Tov paid off the debt, the innkeeper and his family were freed. Of course, the innkeeper immediately invited the Ba'al Shem Tov and his talmidim for a meal in order to thank them.

The Ba'al Shem Tov was always very curious about people, so once he was seated at the innkeeper's table, he asked him, "Please, tell me something about your time in debtors' prison."

The innkeeper shrugged. "What can I say?"

But the Ba'al Shem Tov persisted. "Can't you tell me what it was like?"

The innkeeper shrugged again. "We are happy to be free!"

Still, the Ba'al Shem Tov would not give up, and insisted on finding out more. "How big was the cell? What did it look like? What did they give you and your family to eat? How did you sleep?" He continued questioning the innkeeper until, finally, the innkeeper began talking about his experience.

"Actually, here's something interesting," the innkeeper said. "Every day, from one of the holes that connected my family's cell to the other cells, came some very strange sounds—a lot of crying, sometimes even screaming. This happened all week long, except on Fridays, when we heard tremendous amounts of laughter. All that crying and screaming and laughter was very eerie—and to be honest with you, it scared me and my family—but somehow, we got used to it.

"Then one Friday, we didn't hear anything at all. The silence was even more frightening than the terrible noises. We all huddled together in the cell, as far away from the hole as we could get, until at last we heard a burst of laughter once again. My curiosity got the best of me, and I approached the hole and asked whatever entity had been making those awful sounds, 'Who are you, and why have you gone silent?'

"And the answer I heard was this: 'We are evil spirits belonging to a certain righteous person, a *tzaddik* who lives in a certain city. During the week, this tzaddik fasts and prays, and he never sins. Our sustenance comes from his sins, so all week, we yearn and cry, because he's fasting and praying and doing what he's supposed to do—and he's denying our life force. But every Friday, he decides to break his fast with a big cup of milk—and inevitably, his maidservant knocks over the cup and spills the milk before he can drink it, so this righteous person loses his temper and flies into a rage. At last, he sins, so we evil spirits can exist again, and thrive for another week! That's why, every Friday, we celebrate the return of our life force by dancing and singing, and laughing as loud as we can.'

"But on that day, that silent Friday, when I spoke to the evil spirits," continued the innkeeper, "they had nothing to celebrate—at least not at first. They told me that the tzaddik, who had recognized that his rage was a problem, was trying hard not to sin anymore, so he had locked the cup of milk up in a cabinet. He thought keeping it under lock and key would stop the maidservant from spilling it and throwing him into a temper tantrum. The evil spirits were quiet because they thought they were going to be completely finished.

"But eventually there came a knock at the tzaddik's door. It was the woodcutter, delivering wood for the fire. He needed to be paid, so the tzaddik's wife unlocked the cabinet to get the money. She didn't know the cup of milk was in there, so sure enough, she knocked it over, and the milk spilled, and thus the tzaddik once again went into a rage. The evil spirits got their life force back that day after all, and by nightfall they were laughing and rejoicing again."

As the innkeeper told this story to the Ba'al Shem Tov, one of the talmidim fainted right onto the floor, realizing that this story was about him.

 TEACHING

Redeeming captive families who were thrown into debtors' prison for not paying their rent was a mitzvah that was very close to the Ba'al Shem Tov's heart.

In the *Hayom Yom*, an anthology of Chassidic aphorisms and customs, the Lubavitcher Rebbe writes, "Know that which is above you." He explains the verse as meaning, "That which is above you comes from you." All our actions in this world have an effect. Our rabbis teach us that good actions create a good angel, a positive energy, and negative actions create a bad angel, a negative energy. All of the things that surround us and are above us—the spiritual and the material—arise from ourselves and our actions.

Keeping in mind that each action we take creates a spiritual energy, we can consider everything that we set out to do and ask ourselves, How do I want the energies around me to look?

KING DAVID'S PSALMS

ONCE THERE was a man named Chaim who was a simpleton and one of the water carriers in the city of Mezhbizh, where the Ba'al Shem Tov lived.

Chaim had begun working at a very young age. Although he had not received a formal education, he had been taught the Book of Psalms, and he spent all of his free time reading from it. He knew and loved the book of Psalms so well that he was known throughout Mezhybizh as Reb Chaim the Water Carrier, the *Tehillim Zoget*, or the One Who Says Psalms.

Another man in the city, Reb Ezra Meir, was very wealthy, and he wanted to do something very special for his synagogue. "What could be more special than writing a Torah scroll?" he wondered. But he didn't just want to write a Torah scroll—he wanted to go beyond that, to commission the scroll himself in the best way possible. Reb Meir also wanted to make his Torah scroll extraordinary, to perform *hiddur mitzvah*, the beauty of the mitzvah.

The parchment for all Torah scrolls must come from the skins of kosher animals. But Reb Meir wanted to go above and beyond the general requirement, so he purchased some kosher animals, had them slaughtered in a kosher manner, and donated all their meat to charity. He also made sure that every person who worked on turning the skins into parchment went to the mikveh before doing his work each day. Lastly, Reb Meir hired the most God-fearing scribe he could find, and told him, "Normally, it should take you about six months to write a Torah scroll, but I don't care if it takes you a year, two years, or even three years. Take as long as you need; I want it done in the best way.

This must be the most magnificent Torah scroll ever. I'll pay you for whatever period of time is required for the job."

So the scribe took his time, and after a few years, the Torah scroll was at last completed. As is customary upon its completion, the Torah scroll was sealed and celebrated. Reb Meir began planning a huge feast for many honored guests. He hired Reb Chaim the psalm-sayer to bring water to the party, and serve each of the many tables of guests.

On the night of the party, Reb Meir told Reb Chaim, "Please, don't feel you must only act as a waiter. I want you to enjoy yourself. Feel free to partake in the celebration."

So, as he worked, Reb Chaim began drinking a bit—first one tiny drink, then two little drinks, until he couldn't remember how many drinks of schnapps he'd had. The next thing he knew, he found himself lying on the floor. Reb Meir went over to Reb Chaim, and in front of everybody lost his temper. "I hired you to serve water!" Reb Meir shouted. "I hired you to take care of my guests! And here you are, drunk on the floor!"

Reb Chaim quickly shook off his drunkenness and began apologizing to Reb Meir. "I'm so sorry," he said. "I thought you said to partake, so I partook. I'm so poor, I don't usually drink such strong alcohol. My schnapps is usually watered down, and yours wasn't, so it had a greater effect on me than usual. I apologize. Please forgive me."

But Reb Meir would not accept Reb Chaim's apology, and continued to berate him loudly, humiliating him in front of the guests.

Finally, Reb Meir finished venting his anger, and the party continued. But as Reb Meir approached the podium to address the crowd, a man pulled him aside and said, "Reb Meir, there's someone waiting for you outside, and he says he must talk to you."

"No, no, not now," Reb Meir said impatiently. "I can't. Whoever he is, he has to wait."

The messenger insisted: "No, Reb Meir, it's very, very important that you listen to what this person has to say."

The urgent look on the messenger's face convinced Reb Meir to go outside and enter the carriage that was waiting for him. Inside the carriage, he sat down next to a man he had never seen before.

"Yes? What do you want with me?" Reb Meir asked, but the mysterious man said nothing and the carriage suddenly sped off, traveling very, very quickly. "Where are we going?" Reb Meir asked, but again he got no answer. The next thing he knew, the mysterious man was pushing him out of the carriage, and he found himself alone in a deep forest in the middle of winter.

Since Reb Meir was not dressed for winter, he was absolutely freezing. As he walked along, trying to keep warm, he spotted a light from afar. He ran toward it, and came upon a palace all lit up inside. A party was taking place there, but when he entered the room nobody paid any attention to him. Reb Meir went over to the fireplace and stood warming himself up before the fire. He watched as another guest walked in, and noticed how all the other guests were paying a lot of attention to him. "Oh, Avraham Avinu," they greeted the new guest. "Abraham, our forefather, welcome!"

Then someone else arrived, and the crowd turned to him, calling out, "Isaac, our forefather! Welcome!"

"Now," the people cried, "we are ready to begin." Reb Meir watched as all the guests took their seats at the table. As soon as they were all seated, a man with a long white beard stood up, pointed to Reb Meir, who remained alone at the fireplace, and shouted, "I have a case to bring against him!"

The man continued, "I wrote a book called *Tehillim*, the Book of Psalms. There's a man by the name of Reb Chaim in the city of Mezhybizh who says the psalms in the sincerest way, and it's a beautiful thing to hear. But this Reb Ezra Meir who stands there warming himself by the fire attacked Reb Chaim, and embarrassed and berated him in public. And in doing so, it's as if he berated my book itself, the Book of Psalms."

Suddenly, Reb Meir realized that the person who was speaking was none other than King David himself, and he began to shake with fear. "I want all of you to give a decree against this Reb Ezra Meir for what he did," King David told the people seated at the table. "His attack on the water carrier is an attack on the Book of Psalms itself."

The assembled guests began discussing the situation as Reb Meir watched anxiously. At long last, a man stood up and announced, "I decree that he must die!" The group agreed. "A decree of death!" they shouted. "Capital punishment for him!" Then another man rose from his chair and pointed at Reb Meir, who stood cringing and trembling before the fire, and declared loudly, "This man has offended the Book of Psalms, and disgraced the person who says the Psalms most sincerely, there is no choice but for him to be sent to death."

But King David was sadly shaking his head. "I think that punishment may be a little too harsh," he said. "Shouldn't the individual who sinned be given the opportunity to repent? Let's allow him to return to the party and apologize to the water carrier Reb Chaim for embarrassing him in public."

Everyone around the table listened closely, and then, one by one, they began nodding. "All right," one man said. Then another spoke in agreement: "If we send him back to the party and he apologizes, maybe he shouldn't receive capital punishment."

Just as Reb Meir began to relax, another person at the table stood up—the man from the carriage ride. "I have another complaint to wage against Reb Meir," the mysterious man said. "I live in the same city with him, and he's never once visited me. He also didn't even invite me to his great celebration of the dedication of the Torah." Reb Meir realized with a sinking heart that the man who was speaking was none other than the Ba'al Shem Tov himself.

Shaking with trepidation, Reb Meir somehow managed to cross the room to stand before the group. With his voice quaking from fear and awe, he told King David, Abraham, Isaac, the Ba'al Shem Tov, and all the other members of the group, "Please, I beg of you, give me the opportunity to make up for my sins, to repent for my misdoings. I will not let you down."

No sooner had Reb Meir concluded his promise than he found himself outside of his house again, standing next to the mysterious carriage. His trip to King David's palace, which had seemed to take place over the longest period of time, had turned out to be over in just a few moments. Reb Meir returned to the party, where everyone was still waiting for him to speak. He stepped up to the podium and told the story of what had just happened to him and humbly apologized to Reb Chaim for embarrassing and berating him in public.

The very next day, Reb Meir became a Chassid, a follower of the saintly Ba'al Shem Tov.

TEACHING

This story teaches us about the power of saying the Psalms. The Tzemach Tzedek, the third Lubavitcher Rebbe, teaches that if one knew the power of saying Tehillim and all the commotion and excitement that it causes up in the spiritual worlds, one would not do anything all day but recite the Book of Psalms. It is customary to say a portion of the Psalms each day so that the complete Psalms can be said within a month, and that is a great way to begin reciting Tehillim.

According to Kabbalah, when we carry out an action in this physical world, we create an angel in the spiritual worlds. If the action is good, then we create an advocate, but if we undertake an unholy action, an adversary is created. When we speak aloud the words of the Psalms, we create spiritual angels so intense that they become great advocates for us, both while we are alive and when we pass away.

THE THREE WORLDS

ONE DAY, after the Ba'al Shem Tov completed the services at shul, two men began arguing. The shul, being a place of fellowship, is the last place anyone ever expects to get into a disagreement, let alone witnessing people getting so angry with each that their faces turn purple with rage and they begin threatening each other, which is what two of the Ba'al Shem Tov's followers did that day. One of the men, who happened to be the local fishmonger, screamed at the other man, "I'm so angry I could tear you up, just like I tear up the fish!"

The Ba'al Shem Tov's face turned white with shock. He knew he had to do something right away "Form a circle!" he shouted, and he guided his Chassidim, including the fishmonger and the man he had threatened, to gather together and take hands. When the circle was completed, the Ba'al Shem Tov placed his holy hands onto the shoulders of the men standing on either side of him. Suddenly, it was as if an electrical charge were passing through all of the men, and they jumped and screamed with fright. Right before their very eyes, a terrible vision formed of the fishmonger carrying out his threat, ripping the limbs and tearing the skin from the other man, as if the man were nothing but a fish to be caught, flayed, and sold for someone's dinner. The vision was so real that all the men in the circle, including the fishmonger himself, nearly fainted from terror.

At last the Ba'al Shem Tov removed his hands from the two men flanking him, and the vision ended, but the men were all still frightened. "Let me explain to you what we have just seen," the Ba'al Shem Tov told them. "We have a world of action, a world of speech, and a world of thought. The world of action, the so-called 'real world,' is where we see things happen. But even though something we *say* to one another might not actually take place in the world of action, it does occur in the world of speech. That is what we just witnessed. Similarly, whatever we *think* also actually exists in the world of thought, even if it never happens in the world of action. So we must be careful to have purity of speech, and likewise, purity of thought."

 TEACHING

If we merely think of doing a good deed, God considers that deed as having been done, and we receive a reward, just as if we actually completed the deed.

Let's say I wake up one morning and think, "Today I want to give charity," but for some reason I don't get around to it. Maybe when I walk down the street, the beggar I want to give a dollar to isn't there that day. To God, my thinking about giving a dollar to the beggar is the same as if I handed him money, because my thought still exists in the world of thought even though I didn't bring it to the world of action.

In the same way, when a person speaks—for instance, I might say out loud, "I want to perform a certain mitzvah"—that statement continues to exist in the world of speech. My spoken words create a reality as well. As the Ba'al Shem Tov taught us, we must be as careful with the worlds of speech and thought as we are with our actions on earth, because whatever we say or think exists in their respective worlds. We may not have the sensitivity to realize this, but it is something we should strive to understand and follow.

A Seder without Spiritual Powers

T HE BA'AL Shem Tov once decided to take his family on a journey from their home in Medzhybizh, in Poland, to the land of Israel, but by the time they reached Turkey, he had lost all of his spiritual capabilities. This happened right before Passover, which left the family with no means to make the holiday. The Ba'al Shem Tov knew that the reason he had lost all of his spiritual capabilities was because he was not ever supposed to go to the land of Israel, and therefore going there meant giving up everything. However, his daughter Udel would not give up on her father regaining his spiritual capabilities and their family being able to celebrate the holiday, so she went down to the river to wash her clothing to prepare for Passover anyway. There she noticed a wealthy man who seemed to be Jewish. Udel went over to the man and said, "My father is a great, saintly man, and we are on our way to Israel, the holy land. But we're here for the holiday of Passover and we have nowhere to celebrate. Can we join you?"

The wealthy man gladly invited the Ba'al Shem Tov and his family to join him, and he set up a room for them and took care of them. On the *Seder* night, he did not see anything extraordinary about the Ba'al Shem Tov; in fact, after watching him the whole night, the wealthy man thought, "He seems like a good man, but there's nothing special about him."

On the eve of *Pesach*, we are prohibited from eating bread, nor do we eat matzah, because we want to wait until the Seder night to eat, so that night the Ba'al Shem Tov had nothing to eat or drink except for a single glass of wine, and afterwards, feeling drunk, he fell asleep immediately.

Meanwhile, the wealthy man got ready to go to shul, and when he was about to leave for synagogue, he told Udel, "Please go and wake your father up."

But Udel refused. "I never wake my father when he's sleeping," she said.

So the man went off to synagogue alone. When he returned from shul, he wanted to start the Seder, so once again, he told Udel, "Go and wake your father up." But Udel's response was the same as before: "I never wake my father when he's sleeping."

Feeling impatient, the man decided to go and wake up the Ba'al Shem Tov himself, but when he entered the bedroom, what he saw terrified him. The Ba'al Shem Tov was indeed sound asleep, but as he slept, his face was changing colors: from green to blue, to purple, to red, to orange, to yellow, and back to green. It was so strange and frightening that the man ran from the room. By the time he came upon Udel, he had calmed down enough to tell her that he agreed that they should wait for the Ba'al Shem Tov to wake up himself.

Soon afterward, the Ba'al Shem Tov came out of his room and the Seder began. But when it came to his reading the verse, *to him who performs miracles*, the Ba'al Shem Tov repeated it several times with such fervor and excitement that everyone at the table was gripped with awe. Then he began to tell a story.

"There was once a sultan who wanted to see what was really going in within his kingdom, so he decided to dress as a commoner and visit a few different cities," the Ba'al Shem Tov recounted. "One day, while he was traveling, he was ambushed in the forest by a band of robbers. After the bandits took all his money, they dragged him to the cave where they hid out and told him they were going to kill him.

"The sultan was very smart, and quickly came up with a scheme to save himself: 'Don't kill me! I'm an artist, and I can make art for you to sell for a tremendous amount of money,' he told them. 'But if you kill me, you'll lose out on this chance.'

'What kind of art?' the bandits wanted to know.

"'It's a very unique type of art,' the sultan said. 'In fact, you'll probably go to many art dealers who aren't going to want to touch it. Only a true expert in this field of art will understand it, but when you find him, he will pay you a handsome sum for it.'

"The bandits agreed, so the sultan spent the next few days making a piece of art. When the bandits saw it, they were shocked. 'What kind of art is this?!' they shouted at him. 'This is terrible! Who would possibly want this?' But the sultan promised them the art would fetch a good price, so in the end they decided to try to find a buyer.

"The band of robbers took the piece of art to the nearest city, and went from gallery to gallery, trying to sell it. Every art dealer they met laughed at them and told them it was the worst piece of art they had ever seen, until finally they walked into a gallery owned by a Jew. Unknown to the bandits, the sultan had placed a message within the art saying that he, the sultan, had been kidnapped, but he had carefully disguised part of the message so the bandits wouldn't notice.

"The Jewish gallery owner noticed the message right away and took the piece of art to examine. After having looked it over carefully for a long time, he said, 'Gentlemen, this is a very precious piece of art. What's your price?' The band of robbers named an enormous sum, and to their amazement, the gallery owner went immediately to his safe, took out the money, and paid them. They were even more astonished when, as they left the gallery, the Jewish art dealer told them, 'If you have other pieces of art by this artist, please bring them to me. I'm willing to buy them!'

"The robbers were so excited that once they got back through the woods to their cave, they told the sultan, 'You'd better get cracking and create some more art for us! We've got money to make!'

"So the sultan made a second piece of art containing another message, and the band of robbers took it to the gallery owner, who once again paid them a handsome sum. Then the sultan made a third and a fourth and a fifth piece of art, each one containing messages, until he had conveyed the entire story about how he had disguised himself as a commoner and had been robbed and was now being held captive in a cave in the woods. He had even hidden a message giving the gallery owner the specific location.

"Once the Jewish gallery owner had the whole story, he went to the royal guard and explained what had happened to the sultan. Immediately, the soldiers set off for the cave in the woods, and they saved the sultan.

"When the sultan was back on his throne, he repaid the Jewish art gallery owner for the sums of money he had given to the robbers. But most importantly, the sultan realized not only that the Jews were good people, but that they also faced several challenges in daily life in his kingdom, so he abolished all of the unfair decrees against the Jewish people then and there."

That was the end of the Ba'al Shem Tov's story. But the very next morning at the synagogue, the wealthy man who was hosting the Ba'al Shem Tov's family heard the story of the sultan once again—this time directly from the owner of the art gallery himself.

 TEACHING

In the Torah, there is a verse that calls Israel the land that God's eyes are continually on, from the beginning of the year until the end of the year—meaning there's a higher dimension of spirituality in the land of Israel. Moses's greatest desire was to enter the land of Israel, yet God did not allow it. So, too, the Ba'al Shem Tov's greatest desire was to go to the land of Israel, and yet again, for some reason, his soul was also not permitted to go there. What's very interesting is that the Lubavitcher Rebbe, Menachem Mendel Schneerson, also never went to the land of Israel. Throughout his life, many Israelis asked him, "Why haven't you ever come to Israel? Why don't you join us in the Holy Land?" The Rebbe gave several different answers, but in truth, he was avoiding the question. He would respond, "Well, the Jews in the diaspora need me," or "I need a halachic reason to go," or something of that sort. We see from his answers that the purpose on earth for certain souls is not to go to the land of Israel and tap into that environment of spirituality. Rather their mission is to remain in the diaspora and work on elevating the sparks of godliness that have been lost throughout it.

Regarding the story that the Ba'al Shem Tov tells: Many times, we have to understand that even though we don't have the means of salvation for our particular trouble or challenge, we must maintain *bitachon*—total trust and optimism. We have to have certainty that God will come through for us in a way that may go against logic or what we're conditioned to believe. We have to know that God will come through for us because we had total trust and certainty, bitachon, in Him. Having bitachon is actually even higher than having faith in God.

God always sends healing before the wound, so we need to remember that it actually takes a wound to bring out the healing. The only way we can ever know the strengths we have within us is to be challenged by a wound. If we never are confronted, we will never find out. In order for us to bring out our talents and capabilities, we must be challenged. So, it is with faith—often, we are faced with situations that provoke us to bring out a deeper level of faith and trust in God, one that we would not otherwise know we are capable of having.

The Miser's Thirst

I N THE old country, the wealthiest man of all was also a real miser.
When it came to helping the community, contributing to fundraising campaigns, or giving charity, this man never offered a penny. He
was the cheapest and meanest of people.

One Yom Kippur—the Day of Atonement, on which we all must
fast—with just a few hours left before the end of the holiday this miser
was feeling faint with hunger. So he rushed off to see the rabbi and told
him, "I'm going to faint from hunger! Who knows, maybe I'm even
going to die! I need to eat something right away!"

The rabbi advised him not to give in to the hunger, but to drink
water instead. "If you drink less than an ounce of water at certain inter-
vals, you'll feel better, and it can be considered as if you are continuing
your fast."

So the man started drinking an ounce of water every fifteen minutes. But soon his thirst was even worse than his hunger, and the water
couldn't satisfy him, so he gave up and went back to the rabbi. "Listen,"
he said, "I need to have a full cup of water. I can't drink these little
ounces of water. They're not helping me; they're making me feel worse."

At first the rabbi was not sure what to do. He didn't want to give the
man a halachic ruling without conferring with someone else. The rabbi
went to his rebbe and told him the story. "Rebbe, what should I do?"
the rabbi asked.

"Tell this miser he can drink as many cups of water as he wants
to drink, on the condition that for every cup of water he has to give a
hundred rubles to charity," the Rebbe said.

So the rabbi returned to the miser and said, "Okay, we're allowing
you to drink as much water as you want, but with the stipulation that

you have to give one hundred rubles to charity for each cup that you drink."

The miser thought about it for a moment and then shook his head. "Actually, I'm feeling much better now," he told the rabbi. "I'm not so thirsty anymore."

TEACHING

According to Kabbalah and Chassidut, we each have two souls: an animalistic soul, which gives life to our physical body, and a divine soul, which is a part of God. Our animal soul, or *nefesh habehamit*, is always trying to convince us not to follow Torah and not to perform mitzvot, and it continually presents us with a million ways to break the rules and a million excuses for doing the wrong thing.

Following our nefesh habehamit means going down the wrong path. For instance, throughout the day, whenever we are approached with having to make a choice between taking care of our physical needs or our spiritual needs, we have to ask ourselves: Does my body really need food or water at this moment, or is my nefesh habehamit trying to convince me that I need to eat or drink to keep me away from attaining spirituality?

Here's an example from my own life. I don't eat breakfast on a daily basis. There are six fasting days throughout the Jewish calendar year, but of course, on those days, when I wake up at six o'clock in the morning, I'm already craving something to eat. Obviously, my nefesh habehamit is playing a psychological game with me, trying to convince me that I'm hungry on the one day that I have to fast.

Whenever we experience a physical need, if it's a true need, then we must take care of ourselves. But sometimes, as the Alter Rebbe, the First Chabad Rebbe, taught, it's just the animal soul disguising itself as holy in order to convince us to do something that leads to a place further away from God. It's necessary to learn how to distinguish between the desires of the animal soul and that of the godly soul.

Coffee to Keep Me Awake

ONCE A man by the name of Meir was walking in a certain city when a large group of Chassidim suddenly came running past him. "What's the rush?" Meir called out. "Where are you all running?"

One of the Chassidim stopped and told Meir, "Reb Dovid of Nikolaev, the great Chassidic master, is coming."

"I remember someone named Dovid from Nikolaev," Meir told the man. "He was my study partner many years ago. I wonder if this master is him."

Meir began running, too, following the Chassidim. When he reached Reb Dovid of Nikolaev he saw that, sure enough, it was indeed his old friend.

After the Rebbe finished his discourse he sat down with Meir, who asked him, "When we were study partners together, why did you leave and become a student of the Ba'al Shem Tov?"

"Remember how we always discussed learning Torah for its own sake?" Reb Dovid answered. "Remember we said how good it would be not to learn Torah in order to become great giants in Torah scholarship, or because of any ulterior motive—but instead, simply to study Torah for its own sake? I was told the Ba'al Shem Tov could help me do that, so I went to see him."

"Why didn't you invite me to join you?" Meir inquired.

"I was nervous that you would discourage me from going, so I didn't mention it to you."

"What was it about the Ba'al Shem Tov that made you want to follow him?"

"To tell you the truth," said Reb Dovid, "when I arrived, I wasn't so impressed. Nothing grabbed me. But the Chassidim encouraged me to remain with them through Shabbat. On Friday afternoon, they told me, 'Tonight, when you watch the Ba'al Shem Tov read from the book of the Song of Songs and you hear him sing the verses, he's going to capture your heart.'

"I listened to him, and I admit it was a sublime experience, unlike any I'd ever experienced in my life. However, when it was over, I still was not convinced that I should stay.

"The Chassidim said, 'No, no, no, don't go yet! Why don't you wait to see how the Ba'al Shem Tov prays on the holy day of Shabbat?' So I stayed, and I admit that I had never seen anybody pray like he did, but still I wasn't convinced. On Sunday afternoon, as I was preparing for my journey home, the Chassidim came and told me that there was to be a special occasion that night, that the Ba'al Shem Tov would make a *farbrengen*, a joyous Chassidic gathering. 'If you traveled this far,' they said, 'you may as well stay.'

"I decided to attend, and the Chassidim were delighted. 'Whatever you do,' they warned me, 'make sure not to fall asleep at the farbrengen.'

"I took a long nap that afternoon. As soon as I woke up, I drank a few cups of black coffee. I was all ready to go and felt very sure that I wouldn't fall asleep. I got to the farbrengen early and found a good place at the table, just opposite the Ba'al Shem Tov—an honorable seat.

"When the Ba'al Shem Tov arrived, he washed his hands and began the meal. As we were enjoying the delicious delicacies, he shared a discourse on the meaning and the intentions of the mikveh, the Jewish ritual bath. 'While going to the mikveh is an obligation, a mitzvah, for family purity, for all Jews,' the Ba'al Shem Tov explained, 'the Chassidim go to the mikveh every single day to reach higher spiritual heights.'

"As the Ba'al Shem Tov was concluding his interpretation of the intentions of the mikveh, one of the attendants interrupted him. 'Rebbe,' he called out, 'I don't understand what you're saying. Reb Isaac Luria, the Arizal, gives a different interpretation.'

"Across from me, the Ba'al Shem Tov's face suddenly turned white, as if all the blood drained out of it. Then he closed his eyes, and I felt my body being taken over by slumber. No matter how hard I tried to stay awake, I couldn't help but fall asleep. I found myself up in Heaven with people running all around. 'Why is everybody rushing?' I called out. A man stopped and told me, 'A big debate is about to take place between the Ba'al Shem Tov and the Arizal.' I ran to hear the debate, and when I arrived, the Ba'al Shem Tov was delivering his interpretation of the mikveh and its focus and intentions. After he finished, the Arizal asked him a series of questions, which the Ba'al Shem Tov answered. At the end, everyone, including Reb Isaac Luria, the Arizal, agreed that the Ba'al Shem Tov's interpretation was correct.

"Suddenly, I woke up, and I was back at the farbrengen. I watched the color come back to the Ba'al Shem Tov's face as he began giving his interpretation again to the Chassid who had interrupted him. That individual had not learned from his mistake. Before long, he interrupted the Ba'al Shem Tov again. 'Rebbe, I still don't understand,' he said. 'Reb Isaac Luria, the Arizal, gives a different interpretation.'

"The Ba'al Shem Tov turned to me and said, 'Reb Dovid, maybe you can answer him.' So I told the story of what I had seen take place in Heaven.

"At that farbrengen I knew that my place was with the Chassidim, and I decided to remain and become a student of the Ba'al Shem Tov.'"

TEACHING

In recent times, many farbrengens took place in the Lubavitcher Rebbe's court. Stories are told about individuals who were not religious, not observant, or not properly connected to their heritage attending one of the Lubavitcher Rebbe's farbrengens and reaching a level of spirituality that they had previously never been able to achieve. People said the Rebbe was closer to a godly being than anyone they ever encountered.

In 1979, the Rebbe suffered a major heart attack at the end of the holiday of Simchat Torah. The first public farbrengen he held after his recovery took place about a month later, on Rosh Chodesh Kislev. The Rebbe's cardiologist was against his holding a discourse, but the Rebbe insisted, so the cardiologist agreed to allow him to speak on the condition that his heart would be monitored the entire time. Of course, the monitoring was unbeknownst to the attendees of the farbrengen. To the public, everything looked normal. As was the Rebbe's tradition whenever he delivered Chassidic discourses, he held onto a handkerchief and wrapped it around his hand. Since a Chassidic discourse is given on a very high spiritual level, the person giving the discourse has to hold onto something physical to stay grounded in this world, in the same way that an electrical current needs a grounding wire.

After the farbrengen, the Rebbe's cardiologist said that although the Rebbe's heartbeat throughout the night had been irregular, jumping, and slowing at times, during the time that he shared his Chassidic discourse his heartbeat was perfectly steady.

The Rebbe's story is further evidence that at a farbrengen, one is able to remove many shells, many klipot, and reach a greater depth of connection to the Almighty.

DRINKING MEDICINE

ONCE REB Pinhas of Koritz, a student of the Ba'al Shem Tov, went to visit his colleague, the Maggid of Mezrich—and as he entered the courtyard of the Maggid's house he noticed a piece of paper with some Chassidic teachings written on it blowing across the floor. "Oy vey," Reb Pinhas said to himself as he picked the paper up. "How is it that these holy teachings are scattered on the floor?"

Later on, when Reb Zalman heard about that comment, he recounted a parable:

"Once there was a king whose only son and heir became so sick that the doctors lost all hope, so a specialist was called in from far away to diagnose the prince. The foreign doctor said that the prince could be cured, but only by a special method. 'What you must do,' he advised the royal family's doctors, 'is take the largest diamond, the most precious stone, from the center of the king's crown, grind it up into powder, add some water to it, and feed the prince this mixture, a little bit every day until he is healed.'

"'But the prince is so sick he can't even swallow,' the local doctors objected.

"'That's true,' the doctor said. 'But when you feed him this medication, just count on getting a few drops into his mouth at a time. Don't worry about feeding all of it to him at once. Some of the mixture will spill and be wasted, but the few drops that he ingests will be enough to start the healing. Each time he is fed this medication, he'll be able to ingest a few more drops. In this way, he'll gradually get better until finally he is completely healed.'"

🕎 TEACHING 🕎

This parable is about the teachings of Kabbalah and Chassidut. The Torah's inner dimensions, *Pnimiyut Hatorah*, constitute the most precious part of the study of Torah. The Chassidic teachings are like the beautiful diamond in the center of the king's crown, and because of their long, dark exile, the Jewish people are like the sick child in need of healing. When the diamond is ground up and fed to the sick child, a lot of it spills and is wasted, but a few drops are ingested, and then a few more, and a few more; gradually, all those tiny drops will save the child's life.

The Jewish people are struggling through exile, and they're depressed and not doing well at all. Chassidut, like the diamond in the king's crown, will save them. Like the powdered jewel, Chassidut may be scattered, with many of its teachings lost or not treated with respect. But any Chassidut that is taken in—just like the remaining bits of the diamond powder—will be absorbed to revive the Jewish people. That is why, right now, in this time, it is so important to study the inner dimensions of the Torah.

The Yearlong Indulgence

ONE DAY a Chassidic man went to see his rebbe, and immediately began confessing to him: "Rebbe, I have committed such-and-such a sin and this other sin and yet another kind of transgression...." After he listed all of the sins he had ever committed in his entire adult life, he began pleading with the Rebbe for a path of penitence.

"Rebbe," he said sadly, "I've been indulgent, I've followed so many temptations, and I've given in to all my desires. Please prescribe for me a way of *teshuvah*, of atonement. Please give me a method of repentance so that I can be forgiven."

The Rebbe regarded the man for a moment and then said, "Here's what I want you to do as your atonement: Every morning, sit down to a luxurious breakfast. Eat lots of bread, fish, and cheese. Indulge! Once you're finished eating, just go about your day. When midday arrives, sit down again, and have a lavish lunch. When it comes to dinnertime, enjoy a big feast with meat, delicacies, pasta, vegetables, rice, and desserts—enjoy to your heart's content. Always eat in tremendous luxury. Go out to all of the finest restaurants and really live it up. Do that every single day for one complete year."

The man was rather taken aback by the Rebbe's mode of repentance. However, he told himself, "This is what the Rebbe instructed me, so this is what I must do."

Back at home, on the first day of his atonement, the man prepared himself a luxurious breakfast with many delicacies. As he sat down to consume this feast, he began sobbing. "How is this possible?" he asked himself. "How can it be, for a sinner like me, who chased every temptation and desire in the world, that repentance should mean eating as grandly as this? How can I deserve this?" He cried bitterly, and couldn't put even the smallest morsel of food into his mouth.

When lunchtime and dinnertime arrived that day, the same thing happened: The man painstakingly prepared himself a tremendous meal, and then broke down, shedding copious tears. Because of all his sighing and *krechtzing*, brokenheartedness, and tears, he simply couldn't eat.

Day after day, the same thing happened. The man was careful to prepare one special meal after another, but he could never, ever eat the food. He sobbed from one day to the next and became a broken man. Finally, the long, miserable year was over, and the man returned to his rebbe. Having lost much weight from barely eating, and having such a broken spirit, he arrived looking like a skeleton. Seeing how sad and anguished the man had become, the Rebbe gently said, "I see that you have sincerely repented and returned to God wholeheartedly. You are fully forgiven. Your teshuvah, your penitence, is accepted on high."

TEACHING

Sometimes we simply do not understand the instructions that a rebbe gives us. But we need to remember that rebbes have the power to see into the deepest levels of each person's soul, or neshama. Rebbes also have the power to reconnect us with the *hechste fun di neshama*—the highest and single-most important level of the soul, the Yechidah of the soul, which experiences oneness with God. A rebbe can see and perceive things that the average person cannot. A rebbe knows that what some people might consider to be a reward, such as indulging in the finest foods at every meal, can in fact be a discipline for another person—reawakening and reigniting the person's hechste fun di neshama and reconnecting the person with the Almighty.

The Shabbat Recipe

REBBE YEHUDAH HaNasi, who is often referred to as Rebbe Yehudah the Prince, is best known for redacting the Mishnah, the first part of the Talmud. He was born into a very wealthy family about eighty years after the destruction of the Second Temple, and not only was he the leader of the Jewish people at that time, but he was a very good friend of the Roman ruler of Judea.

One Shabbat afternoon, the ruler was passing by Rebbe Yehudah's home and decided to drop in and pay him a visit. Rebbe Yehuda was about to sit down to his Shabbat lunch, so he invited the ruler to join him, and the ruler was happy to join him.

At Rebbe Yehuda HaNasi's table, the ruler found himself enjoying the most wonderful dish he had ever tasted. It was so delicious that as soon as he returned to his palace, he went directly to his chef and asked if he could replicate it. "The dish that I just had at Rebbe Yehuda HaNasi's house was extraordinary—I've never had anything like it in my life!" he told the chef. "I want you to go to his chef immediately and get the recipe and make that dish for me."

So, the ruler's chef went to meet with Rebbe Yehuda HaNasi's chef, took notes on the recipe, and returned to the palace in time to prepare the dish for the ruler that very evening.

But when the ruler tasted the dish, he rose from the table in anger and called in his chef. "These are not the same delicacies that I tasted at the home of the Rabbi," he told him.

The next day, the ruler's chef went back to Rebbe Yehuda HaNasi's house to meet with the Rebbe's chef again. He checked the list of ingredients and took more notes—and even practiced cooking the dish. Then he went back to the palace and prepared the recipe once again.

But when the ruler sat down to eat, he still wasn't happy with the dish. "It's similar," he said, "but the flavor just isn't the same."

So, the ruler's chef returned to meet with Rebbe Yehuda HaNasi's chef for a third time, and then a fourth time, but each time he prepared the dish the ruler got up and left the table, dissatisfied.

"Why isn't your dish as good as the dish I ate at Rebbe Yehuda HaNasi's house?" the ruler demanded. But the chef had no answer.

The ruler was so frustrated that he called Rebbe Yehuda HaNasi himself to come to his court. "Rabbi, I don't understand what's happening," he said as the Rebbe stood before him. "You served me a dish that I loved, so my chef got the recipe from your chef, but every time my chef makes it, it's different from what you served me. Why isn't my chef's dish as good as yours?"

"Ah," Rebbe Yehuda said. "That's because there was one ingredient that was in my dish that wasn't included in your dish."

"Share it with me!" the ruler demanded.

"No," the Rebbe said. "I can't do that."

The ruler turned bright red with anger. "What do you mean—you can't do that?"

"Because, you see," Rebbe Yehuda said gently, "this ingredient is very hard to come by."

"No problem!" shouted the ruler. "I have all the money in the world, and all the power in the world. I can buy that ingredient, wherever it comes from."

"No, you can't," Rebbe Yehuda said. "This mysterious ingredient is the taste of Shabbat. The holy Sabbath day gives a certain special flavor to all that we cook and gives us a special enjoyment of all that we eat. The ingredient you're looking for cannot be mimicked, or purchased, or found anywhere but in the observance of the holy Shabbat day."

🕎 TEACHING 🕎

If we respect and cherish the Shabbat the way we should, then the Shabbat will bring with it many great delights, or pleasures. These delights enhance everything—from our Shabbat meal, to our family relationships, to life itself. The delights of the Shabbat uplift us and, as we read in the Zohar, bring blessings to the entire week ahead. And if you did not grow up being observant and you begin the journey of even some of the Shabbat observances, you will immediately experience Shabbat delights. Here is one easy way to begin:

On Friday nights, we light two candles. One is for the honor of Shabbat and the other is for the pleasure of Shabbat. As the Chabad rabbis teach us, if the Jewish people keep two Sabbaths properly, immediately, they will be redeemed. Many people understand this as two consecutive Saturdays, or Sabbaths. But there is a Chassidic discourse by Reb Shneur Zalman of Liadi that essentially says, "When we're saying they keep two Sabbaths, we're not referring to two consecutive weekends, but rather we're referring to two levels of spirituality." For example, when we talk about the awe of God or the love of God, there is a lower level and a higher level. On the lower level of love for God, some aspect of the ego exists. On the higher level of love, the ego doesn't exist. On the lower level, I love my life and I know that my life comes from God, so I love God. But on the higher level of love, I don't care if I exist or not; I just want to be attached to God.

Jewish mysticism teaches us that we can experience the phenomenon of the spiritual world within the physical world to the extent that we can be changed by it. When we create the proper channels, we can change the physical world, but this depends on the individual who must draw down the light of God from the highest of spiritual levels to the lowest physical level.

The Joy of the Chassidim

WHY THE REBBE LAUGHED

ONE FRIDAY night, during Shabbat dinner, no sooner had the challah been sliced than the Ba'al Shem Tov burst out laughing. It was so sudden and unexpected that nobody at the table knew what to think of it. Everything was quiet until everyone had finished the fish course and the soup was about to be served—and then the Ba'al Shem Tov began laughing again, this time even more heartily than the first time. And, when the meat course was being served, he fell into yet another fit of laughter.

Of course, everybody at the table was curious to know what was so funny, but nobody had the audacity to approach the Ba'al Shem Tov directly. Instead, they asked Reb Zev Kitzes, who was one of the Rebbe's favorite famous students, to find out why the Rebbe had laughed so hard.

That Saturday night, as the Ba'al Shem Tov sat drinking his tea, Reb Zev plucked up his courage and asked him, "Rebbe, what made you keep laughing so mysteriously during Shabbat dinner?"

"Let's go for a ride," the Ba'al Shem Tov responded.

So Reb Zev and the other Chassidim piled into the Ba'al Shem Tov's horse-drawn carriage. "Whip the horses!" the Ba'al Shem Tov instructed his drunken driver, Alexa. "Let them take us where they may!" As always, as soon as the horses took off Alexa fell fast asleep, and the horses raced all through the night, guided by God.

The next morning, the horses pulled the carriage into the *shtetl* of Koznitz and the Ba'al Shem Tov and the Chassidim went straight to the local synagogue. After leading the congregation in prayers, the Ba'al Shem Tov called for a certain person to come forward. Immediately, a man stepped out of the crowd to stand before the Ba'al Shem Tov.

"Go call your wife to appear before me," the Ba'al Shem Tov said, and the man did as he was told.

When the couple stood together in front of him, the Ba'al Shem Tov asked them, "How did you conduct yourself Friday night?"

The man and his wife immediately broke down in tears. "Oh, Rebbe," the man cried, "if we have sinned, please tell us, and we promise we will follow any mode of atonement that you prescribe for us!"

"What happened on Friday?" the Ba'al Shem Tov asked again.

"I'm a bookbinder, and I'm getting on in years," the man began. "To be honest, business isn't so great lately. When Friday came, there wasn't any money to make the Shabbat meal, so I told my wife we would have to do without it. 'Listen,' I said to her, 'until now, we've never taken any charity nor have we accepted money from the public funds, and I don't want to start doing that now.'

"Every Friday I go to synagogue early, and as is my custom, I read the verses of the Book of the Song of Songs. Last time, when shul was over, I knew I had nothing to go home for—because we had no food, no candles to light, no wine for the *Kiddush*, no challah to break, nothing for Shabbat—and that made me sad, so I *kratzed*, procrastinated, for a while.

"Finally, it was late, and I set out for home with a heavy heart. But as I approached the house, what should I see but candles burning in the windows! When I walked in, I found that not only were there candles burning, but our table was laden with food and wine. What's all this, I thought. I didn't know what to make of it, but I sang the customary song of welcoming the angels into our home for Shabbat and then I stood at the table with my wife and began to say Kiddush over the wine. While I was saying Kiddush, I thought to myself—I know what's happened. My wife couldn't handle not celebrating Shabbat, so she must've gone to borrow money from the neighbor—or even worse, maybe she's taken money from charity!

"What could I do? I couldn't blame my wife for wanting to make the holy Shabbat day special. So after I finished saying Kiddush, I looked over at her and I told her, 'I forgive you.'

"But she said, 'No, no, no! Before you say anything, you have to listen to me. I know that you told me you'd never take charity, and that's it. I agreed with you. I decided I would clean the house all day. Even if we couldn't celebrate Shabbat, the house would be sparkling, befitting the Shabbat Queen.'"

At this point, the bookbinder paused for a moment, and hung his head. "Rebbe," he told the Ba'al Shem Tov, "we don't really own much of anything at all. But my wife told me, 'While I was cleaning, I found in the closet the beautiful pair of gloves you bought me early in our marriage. On the gloves were sterling silver buttons. I took the silver buttons off the gloves and I brought them to the pawn shop and cashed them in. Then I rushed off to the marketplace. There I bought fish and chicken and candles and wine. Everything on this table has come from the money I made from the sale of the silver buttons—everything you see before you!'

"I was so pleased and excited," said the bookbinder, "that I stood up and grabbed hold of my wife and danced around the table with her. And then we sat down and had the fish course. It was so delicious that after we finished it, I jumped up and grabbed my wife and danced with her again. We were both laughing with joy. After the soup course, I still felt so happy that I got up and danced a third circle around the table, for I was filled with such delight and so much gratitude that there was simply nothing else to do but dance."

Looking very sad, the bookbinder turned to face everyone in the room. "If I have sinned, I'm truly sorry," he told the Ba'al Shem Tov and the crowd. "Rebbe, please give me a mode of penitence. I'll do whatever you say."

The Ba'al Shem Tov turned to his Chassidim and said, "When I laughed on Friday night at our Shabbat dinner it was because when this couple got up and danced, they caused such tremendous joy to the Creator." He then turned to the bookbinder and his wife and said, "Because you caused such pleasure up on high, I'm going to give you a blessing. Would you prefer a blessing for riches or a blessing for a child?"

The bookbinder and his wife looked at each other for a moment and then the bookbinder said, "Rebbe, we're in our older years, and we have never been blessed with children. We would like to have a child."

The Ba'al Shem Tov blessed them, and told them, "You're going to have a child within the next year, and when he is born you must notify me because I am going to be the *sandek*, the one to hold the baby during the circumcision. You must name the child Yisrael (Israel) after me."

Sure enough, less than a year later, the older couple had a son whom they named Yisrael, and the Ba'al Shem Tov was the boy's sandek. That child grew up to become the great Chassidic master known as the Maggid of Koznitz.

TEACHING

In Chassidut and Kabbalah, there is the concept of *simcha shel mitzvah*, which literally means "the joy of the mitzvah." We are to serve God with joy. When we perform a mitzvah, we must do it in a joyful manner and feel true happiness while we are performing it.

On a deeper level, our happiness must arise from the fact that we have this opportunity to fulfill a mitzvah. Essentially, the purpose of any mitzvah is to connect to God. In *Perkei Avot*, or *Chapters of Our Fathers* (a compilation of Rabbinical Jewish traditional ethical teachings), it is explained that the reward for a mitzvah is the mitzvah itself. Performing the mitzvah should bring tremendous joy to us simply for the fact that we had the opportunity to do a good deed and connect to the Almighty.

A Taste of Eden

REB DAVID of Lvov was a student of the Rebbe Yaakov Yitzchak, the *Chozeh* (or seer) of Lublin. But Reb David lived far away from his rebbe, and since he did not like to travel alone to visit, he asked his friend to accompany him. Before the two men departed for their long journey, the friend's wife cooked them a meal to see them off.

Once Reb David returned home after visiting the Rebbe, he told his wife all about his travels, including the meal that he had eaten at his friend's house right before they left. "It was so great, it tasted like the Garden of Eden," he remarked. "It was a meal the likes of which I have never had in my entire life." The *Rebbetzin* was puzzled. Her husband had never before complimented her on her own cooking, and now, here he was, complimenting someone else's wife! "It's not like him to go out of his way to tell me how delicious another woman's meal is," she thought. "All right," she told her husband, "let me go and ask her what she made so I can make it for you."

The next morning, the Rebbetzin walked to the home of her husband's friend to talk to his wife. "So, what did you cook for my husband?" she demanded. The friend's wife said, "To tell you the truth, we're very poor, and I had nothing in the house but flour. I didn't even have any firewood, so I went into the woods and collected a few twigs. Then I put on a pot of water to boil, and I took the flour, mixed it into the water, boiled it up, and served it to them," she said.

"But since Reb David of Lvov, the holy tzaddik, the saintly Rebbe, was coming to my house, I knew I couldn't just give him flour and water, because that would be disrespectful. And I didn't even have any salt or oil to add to the dough. So I prayed like this: '*Ribono Shel Olam*, Master of the Universe, I know that you have stored away the Garden of Eden's delicious delicacies. Since I must feed this tzaddik and I have nothing to give him, please make this flour and water taste just like the Garden of Eden.'"

 TEACHING

Certain people are more attuned to their godly soul and spiritual existence than they are to their physical existence. When they taste well-prepared food, they don't necessarily notice all of the food's flavors and seasonings. But when they taste bland food made by a cook who was experiencing spiritual joy while cooking, they're able to taste a spark of godliness.

When we eat, are we sensitive enough to taste the spark of godliness within the food, or are we only focused on the food's superficial qualities: its textures, flavors, seasonings, and spices?

A GIFT FOR THE REBBE

O NE YEAR, on the holiday of Purim in the city of Kozhnitz in what is now Poland, a man by the name of Chaim'ke came from a tiny village nearby for the reading of the *Megillah, The Scroll [book] of Esther*, by the Maggid Reb Yisrael Hopstein, who was also known as the Maggid of Kozhnitz.

As soon as the reading of the Megillah was completed, the Maggid, who was in a very festive mood, approached the Chassid and asked him, "Why didn't you bring me a *mishloach manot*?" The Maggid was referring to the special commandment that we must fulfill on the holiday of Purim: to give special baskets of food to all of our friends. "Why didn't you bring me the gift?" the Maggid kept asking.

Chaim'ke didn't know what to say. "Bring the Maggid food?" he thought to himself. "Back at home, my children and my wife are starving! How can I bring gifts to my Rebbe, the great Maggid of Kozhnitz?" He stood silently before the Rebbe, feeling embarrassed.

The Maggid continued to study Chaim'ke. Finally, he spoke again. "You know what, it's Purim anyway, with or without gifts," he said. "It's okay that you didn't bring me mishloach manot. You can bring it to me next year. In the meantime, come to my house now, and make a *l'chaim* with me."

Off the two of them went to the Maggid's house, feeling joyful in the spirit of Purim, and together they made a l'chaim (a toast) for the festive day. When Chaim'ke said goodbye to the Maggid, he promised to bring him mishloach manot the following year. Then he set off for his village, feeling a little tipsy. As he walked down the street, he spotted a wine store. In the spirit of Purim, he walked in and greeted the shopkeeper happily. "Happy Purim! How are you today?" he said. "You know what? Let me get a bottle of wine. Put it on my tab. You know I'm good for it."

Since the little shop owner was also in especially good spirits for the holiday, he gave Chaim'ke a bottle of wine on credit. Afterwards, Chaim'ke went next door to the bakery and asked the baker for a nice loaf of *mandelbrot*, almond bread. The baker was also in a good mood because of the holiday, so he gave him a loaf on credit as well. Then Chaim'ke marched back to the Maggid's house and presented him with the bottle of wine and the loaf of mandelbroit as a mishloach manot gift for Purim.

The Maggid was surprised, and very pleased, but Chaim'ke had some misgivings about what he had just done. "Oh my God," he thought. "I just borrowed money to give the Maggid a gift, and my children still have no food at home!"

But he was still filled with the holiday spirit, so he went back into the wine store and picked up another bottle of wine on credit, and returned to the bakery for a loaf of challah. Then he stopped at the fish store, too, and bought a few herrings. And, carrying the wine and bread and fish in his arms, he marched joyfully all the way home.

"Happy Purim, everybody!" he called out as he arrived at home with the food. Immediately, his family began making a festive party for the holidays. His wife and children had gone without food for such a long time that, as they enjoyed the feast Chaim'ke had brought home, they repeatedly jumped up from the table and began dancing and singing.

All of a sudden, there was a knock at the door. "It's probably the neighbors," Chaim'ke told his wife. "They must be able to hear us celebrating, and now they're coming to steal our food. Don't open the door!" But his wife peeked out the window to see who it was, and recognized the man. "Don't worry, it's not anybody trying to cause us trouble," she told her husband. "It's our friend Ivan." And she opened the door.

There stood Ivan on their doorstep, bruised and bleeding.

"Ivan, tell me, what's wrong?" Chaim'ke's wife asked, but Ivan was so badly injured he couldn't even speak. Obviously, something terrible had happened to him, so the family brought Ivan inside and dressed his wounds. Then they sat him in a chair by the fire so he could warm up and have a little supper.

After a while, when Ivan had finally come back to himself again, he told them, "My son beat the living daylights out of me and threw me out of my own house. But you, my neighbors, took good care of me. I cannot tell you how grateful I am."

After spending a few days in their home, healing his wounds and getting a little bit more mobile, Ivan told Chaim'ke, "Come with me." He limped his way into the forest with Chaim'ke following behind him, until they came to the place where Ivan said he had hidden something. "This is my life savings, my treasure," Ivan said. "I see that my son hates me. After the way he treated me, I'm not giving it to him. I'm giving it to you. When I die, you'll inherit it."

Sure enough, a few months later, Ivan passed away, and Chaim'ke went out into the forest and dug up the secret treasure. The Chassid and his family inherited Ivan's wealth, and every year after that, Chaim'ke was able to fulfill his promise to give the great Maggid of Kozhnitz, his Rebbe, a gift of mishloach manot on the holiday of Purim.

TEACHING

When it comes to the shattering of all boundaries, there is no greater ingredient than *simcha*, pure joy. When we experience simcha, we are able to accomplish anything to which we put our minds, and we can break through any barrier or limitation within the physical world. Simcha gives us the power to achieve new heights and do things we wouldn't normally feel comfortable doing. That's why, when you're at a celebration, people who normally aren't physically affectionate will sometimes give you a big hug and a kiss. People do this in moments of simcha that take them beyond their normal comfort zone and break through their limitations.

SITTING IN MY PLATE OF FOOD

BEFORE THE Holy Grandfather, or *Saba Kadisha*, became famous as a Chassidic master, he and his wife were extremely poor.

One year, just after the solemn day of Yom Kippur had passed and the joyous holiday of Sukkot was about to begin a few days later, the Holy Grandfather and his wife still had no money and very little food on hand. Nevertheless, they faithfully followed the Sukkot traditions and built a sukkah, a hut, in which to sit to enjoy celebratory meals together.

On the first day of Sukkot, the Holy Grandfather went off to synagogue to pray, and when he returned to the sukkah, he was shocked to find the table laden with a beautiful loaf of freshly baked challah and a fish cooked to perfection.

"What's all this?!" he cried. It turned out that his wife had sold off one of her pieces of jewelry so that she could buy the food to prepare a proper meal for their Sukkot table. The Holy Grandfather was so hungry, and so pleased and excited, that he snatched up the full goblet of wine and sang the Kiddush blessing beautifully over it. Then he grabbed the challah and lifted it up and recited the *HaMotzi* blessing with zeal. After tearing off a piece of challah, he began stuffing the bread into his mouth, chewing and swallowing with great gusto.

Next, the fish was served, and the Holy Grandfather ate it so quickly and with such joy and enthusiasm that he nearly swooned. But then, he slammed down his knife and fork and stopped eating altogether. "Where am I?" he wondered. "Am I sitting in a sukkah? Is this how somebody behaves on the first night of Sukkot?"

He sat silently for a long moment, thinking about the surprise of the meal, how happy it had made him, and how he had been eating so rapidly. Then he announced, "I will not take another bite of this wonderful dinner."

"But why?" his wife asked in amazement.

"Because," the Holy Grandfather explained, "when I ate tonight, I found that I was no longer sitting in my sukkah. I was sitting directly in my dish. I was sitting right in the food itself!"

TEACHING

Sometimes we are so hungry that when we finally get to eat, we do it zealously. But if we partake of food in a *chazarous* (piggish) manner, then we've got a big problem. Then we're not just eating, we're so focused on the food that we're almost turning into the food itself. When we eat, we need to be careful to remain aware of the higher power of eating. Food is a miraculous thing, so we have to eat in a godly manner, in order to elevate the godly spark within the food. If we don't eat in a godly manner, it's as if we are sitting right in the food itself.

This story about the Holy Grandfather reminds me of another story about the Ba'al Shem Tov. One day, as he sat in a *kretshme*, or tavern, with the members of the Chevraya Kadisha, his holy society, he noticed a man at the next table who was eating and eating and eating, completely oblivious to everyone and everything else in the place—unaware even of himself. "Quick!" the Ba'al Shem Tov told his followers. "Hold hands and form a circle!" As soon as the Ba'al Shem Tov and his followers gathered and touched their hands together, what did they see at the next table? Not a man, but a steer, gluttonously eating a steak!

Bringing Healing through Food

YECHIEL ZLOTCHOV was a follower and adherent of the holy Ba'al Shem Tov, as well as a man of great stature and a Chassidic master. Reb Yechiel's own father, Reb Yitzchok, had studied, as was common back then, in a *kollel*, a yeshiva that was supported by the local philanthropists. Essentially, the philanthropists in a town would take a number of families—perhaps ten or even twenty—and support those families as they occupied themselves fully with the study of Torah and the pursuit of spirituality and godliness. The philanthropists would cover all of the families' living expenses so that the men could sit in study all week long. This relationship was called *yissacher* and *zevulan*—while one partner prayed and studied Torah, the other partner pursued business opportunities, and both were obliged to fill the needs of the other and share in the rewards.

While Reb Yitzchok was studying Torah in a kollel as part of a yissacher and zevulan partnership, the local philanthropist's daughter became very ill. The philanthropist, rather than trying to arouse mercy from Heaven on his own, went to the yeshiva carrying a big bag of money, which he divided up and handed out to every member of the group.

He told the members of the yeshiva, "Here's some extra money for your families this week in honor of the speedy recovery of my daughter." Everyone at the yeshiva went home and began fasting and praying for compassion from on high for the girl. Reb Yitzchok took his money home to his wife and told her, "Use this money to throw a huge feast, as if it's a holiday. Go and buy some challah, some fish, and some meat. Let's make a big celebration." His wife did as she was asked, and that evening, Reb Yitzchok and his family held a great feast. They served their many guests a great variety of delicacies, and everyone was very festive.

A few days later, the philanthropist returned to the yeshiva and announced that his daughter had miraculously healed. At hearing this news, the other students became a little resentful of Reb Yitzchok. After all, they had been fasting and praying, and they had helped the philanthropist's daughter get better, but what had he done? He had been frivolous, eating and drinking and celebrating. He hadn't helped with the philanthropist's daughter's recovery at all. This bothered the yeshiva group so much that they paid a visit to the philanthropist's house to tell him about it.

Soon afterward, the philanthropist held a *seudat hoda'ah*, a feast of thanksgiving, to thank the Almighty for bringing healing to his daughter. At the feast, after drinking a little l'chaim, the philanthropist invited Reb Yitzchok to sit down with him. "I know you're a man of great stature," said the philanthropist, "so why is it that while my daughter was very ill and everybody else was praying and fasting for her recovery, you took the money and used it to make a feast and hold a celebration?"

"Actually, it's very simple," Reb Yitzchok answered. "Had I prayed and fasted, then that would've meant nothing in Heaven because I pray and fast all the time. Since I ate a huge feast, up in Heaven they were all talking about it. 'Why is Yitzchok celebrating?' they were asking. 'Oh, is he eating because the local philanthropist gave him charity? And why did the donor give extra charity to all the students this week? Because his daughter is ill? Well, in the merit of this extra charity, we should bring healing to his daughter!' So, actually, my eating instead of fasting brought about such delight up in Heaven that your daughter was healed."

 TEACHING

We're conditioned to believe that living like an ascetic—praying and refraining from eating all day long—is the best way to attract the mercy of the Almighty. But whoever said that conventional thinking is always correct? It's true that there are designated days to fast, but at times, it's possible that, done in the right context, we can bring about the same healing and compassion from the Almighty through eating and festivity. For instance, our rabbis teach us that if we eat a festive meal on the eve of Yom Kippur and then fast on the day of Yom Kippur, it is as if we fasted two days in a row. Eating can accomplish the same desired outcome as fasting.

In Chabad Chassidism, there is a text called "The Letter of Repentance," which discusses the concept of fasting and what it accomplishes. Fasting in itself does not bring about atonement or forgiveness, but it can arouse a level of brokenheartedness by weakening the physical body, and thus the person's ego as well, which ultimately inspires the person to repent. In this way, fasting is holy.

Fasting that makes oneself too weak to study Torah or do good deeds is not holy. The same is true when it comes to eating—overindulging to the point of making oneself feel too ill to study or perform mitzvot is not holy. But if one eats in the right context, one is able to accomplish as much, if not more, than what can be done by fasting.

Stale Bread and Water

In Old Europe, when a girl reached marriageable age, her father would search for a suitable groom for her. Once the couple had met and were certain that they liked each other, they would get married. Often the bride's father would support them for a few years to allow his son-in-law to study Torah.

Since there was a large antagonistic movement against the Chassidim in those days, it was common for a Chassidic son-in-law not to tell his father-in-law that he belonged to the Chassidic movement. If the father-in-law eventually found out, he would often give his Chassidic son-in-law a lot of grief and torment.

Such was the case of Reb Moshe of Kobrin, who later became a Chassidic master. His father-in-law was extremely cruel to him, so much so that Reb Moshe was only given a few morsels of stale bread and a little water each day, and he practically starved. Because of that, he was always physically exhausted and had a very weak constitution. To make matters worse, his father-in-law would send him out to do tasks requiring a lot of physical labor, like picking up goods he had bought in the marketplace and schlepping the heavy items for him.

When the holiday of Hoshanna Rabbah came, Reb Moshe had to do all the schlepping for his father-in-law once again, but he was looking forward to the nice festive meal he was accustomed to having on that day, so he was able to find the strength to complete all of his tasks. That day, he arrived at the sukkah feeling very hungry but also happy, but all he found there were a few pieces of stale bread and some sour milk. Nonetheless, he and his wife ate the meal with joy. Afterwards, he donned his festive clothing and made his way to synagogue to join in the *hakafot*, dancing joyfully in a circle around the Torah, on the holidays of Shimini Atzeret and Simchat Torah. Despite being hungry, tired, and weak, he still felt joyful to be dancing at the celebration.

Later in life, Reb Moshe recalled that particular Simchat Torah as one of the most joyous ones of his life.

 TEACHING

One of Judaism's fundamental principles and teachings that the holy Ba'al Shem Tov emphasized is *ivdu et Hashem b' simcha*: serve God with joy. Our happiness should never depend on the physical situation or the material or financial position in which we find ourselves. No matter how rich or poor we are, we must always strive to serve the Almighty with joy. If our joy and jubilation is based on materialism, then we have developed an appetite that can never be satisfied. Ultimately, someone who is truly rich is someone who is happy with his or her lot. As we read in *Chapters of Our Fathers*, riches are measured not by how much we amass, but by the satisfaction we have with the blessings that we have received.

HERSCHEL THE GOAT LOVER

ONE DAY, while the Ba'al Shem Tov was still a secret mystic, he was out walking in the marketplace with some of his companions when he noticed a man walking alone at a distance, surrounded by an aura of light. The man shone so brightly that it was as if he had swallowed the sun, and the Ba'al Shem Tov immediately set out across the marketplace to meet him. But by the time he got to the other side, the man had disappeared.

The next day the Ba'al Shem Tov made sure to arrive at the marketplace earlier. Sure enough, there was the man again, standing in the same place, shining like gold. "That must be a really righteous person," the Ba'al Shem Tov told the other mystics, and he went off to follow the man through the marketplace. He watched as the man, who was dressed in tattered clothing, selected the greenest, freshest greens to buy, breaking off a tiny piece of each one to taste before he chose it and placing the selected produce into a very fancy tote bag.

After the man finished his shopping, the Ba'al Shem Tov followed him all the way to the outskirts of a village, to the tiny shack the man called home. Standing on the street and looking through the open front door, the Ba'al Shem Tov could see that the man's house was filled with goats. He watched as the man set his beautiful bag of greens on the table, and the goats gathered around, bleating. Then the man fed the goats the tender herbs, petting each goat as it had its fill, and he was licked with affection in return. The Ba'al Shem Tov was so touched and puzzled by this scene that he returned very late that night to the shack to investigate and found the man sleeping on the bare floor with the goats lying on top of him like a blanket.

The next morning, during his visit to the marketplace, the Ba'al

Shem Tov asked everyone who greeted him, "Who is that man with the goats, the one who shines so brightly?" And the people shrugged and said, "Oh, that guy? He's Herschel the Goat Lover. He sure loves his goats!" But this explanation hardly satisfied the Ba'al Shem Tov's curiosity. It didn't make sense to him at all that a man who dressed in tattered clothing, lived in a shack, took care of goats, and did nothing else should be enveloped in an aura of light.

After following Herschel for two more days, the Ba'al Shem Tov still couldn't make sense of him. Finally, he cornered Herschel in an alleyway and demanded, "Tell me your secret!"

"But I don't have a secret," Herschel said.

"You must have a secret! Tell me what it is!"

"No, no secret," Herschel said. "I'm just a simple man."

"All right then," the Ba'al Shem Tov relented. "Please, just tell me your life story."

So Herschel sat down in the alleyway with the Ba'al Shem Tov and began.

"I was married to a very, very holy woman, who spent her time taking care of the poor and the sick," he said. "But, sadly, she passed away at a young age. After she died, she came to me in a dream and told me that I had to keep doing what she had done—take care of the hungry and the sick. I wanted to honor her by fulfilling her command—but, at first, I didn't know how to do it properly. All I knew was that I owned goats. So I began keeping these goats very well. I feed them the choicest food and give them the best life they could possibly have. In return, they produce for me the highest-quality goat milk. Every night, I go to the local synagogue and check the list of people needing prayers to find out who's sick or injured, who just gave birth, and who's recovering from surgery. And then, when everyone is sleeping, I go out and secretly leave a jug of goat milk on each of their doorsteps. I know my milk brings them healing."

When the Ba'al Shem Tov heard this story, he understood why Herschel had such a bright aura, and he was so moved by Herschel's story that he invited him to join his society of holy mystics. The Ba'al

Shem Tov himself taught Herschel how to read and educated him so that Herschel eventually became a great mystic.

 TEACHING

Unfortunately, in our ambitious, materialistic society, we tend to look down on simple tasks. We think, "I'm too important or distinguished to do that," or even "I'm too holy to do that." But when you look at simple tasks from the perspective of godliness, you can see what is really holy: An impoverished person like Herschel, wearing tattered clothing, living in a shack at the edge of a city—taking care of his animals with the sincere intention of using their milk to help the sick, the hurt, and the downtrodden. Herschel the Goat Lover's whole existence, from morning to night, might have been strange, but he lived that way so he could produce the greatest quality of milk to bring about healing to other people. His life was a true example of *tahavak yisrael* (love of thy neighbor).

Ultimately, our mission in this world is to help other people, and we can each do so in our own way. The Ba'al Shem Tov teaches that each of us may be put on the earth for seventy or eighty years just to do one single favor for another person. Herschel dedicated his entire life to helping people, and that is why he was surrounded by the brightest possible aura of light.

Bring the Tea

THIS STORY is told in the book, *A Treasury of Chassidic Tales: On the Torah,* by Rabbi Shlomo Yosef Zevin.

The famous Rebbe Yitzchok Isaac of Zidatsov had a grandson, Yaakov Yitzchok Chozeh, who later became the Rebbe of Chadorov. But when Yaakov Yitzchok Chozeh was still a young man, he suddenly fell ill and was in danger of dying.

The young man's family members were all beside themselves with worry and sorrow. They rushed to Rebbe Yitzchok Isaac and told him, "*Zadie*, Grandpa, your grandson is now on his deathbed." Shocked by the news, the Rebbe locked himself into his study and began praying desperately, begging God to please help his grandson recover.

The situation only turned from bad to worse. The family members became terribly upset and wanted to tell the Rebbe what was happening, but they were afraid to disturb his prayers. At first, they couldn't figure out what to do, but then they decided to send in the Rebbe's great-grandson, Yehuda Tzvi, who would later grow up to become the Rebbe of Dolinov, to disturb the Rebbe with the bad news about the sad state of his grandson.

The young Yehuda knocked on the Rebbe's door, and was welcomed into his Zadie's study. However, the boy didn't deliver the bad news as he had been instructed. Instead, he put it to his great-grandfather this way: "Zadie, you should know that your grandson Yaakov Yitzchok Chozeh is doing a lot better now. So please pray to God that he continues with his full and speedy recovery."

Upon hearing this, Rebbe Yizchok Isaac jumped straight out of his chair and also out of his somber mood. With a huge smile on his face, the Rebbe rushed to his cupboard, grabbed a box of tea leaves, and handed it to Yehuda. "Give the patient this tea," he said. "Once he drinks it, everything will be all right."

A few hours later, the patient was able to take a few sips of the tea, and the family noticed that at last he had taken a turn for the better. Ever so slowly, he began to improve. But his recovery was not steady, and a few days later, he suffered a setback. This time the adults in the family went straight to talk to Rebbe Yitzchok Isaac themselves. "Zadie, he's gotten worse," they told him, their voices all very distraught. "He's taken a step backwards. Whatever can we do?"

Rebbe Yitzchok Isaac sat listening to them, shaking his head the whole time. "Listen," he told them, "you shouldn't have let me know like this. You should have told me in a more joyful way. God forbid that this should ever happen again; if it does, please take a lesson from the little one, Yehuda. Instead of putting me in a place of hopelessness and melancholy, he made me feel hopeful about the situation. Because of Yehuda, I prayed to God with a lighter, more joyful heart, and therefore I was able to bring about a blessing that was both greater and faster."

TEACHING

Often we find ourselves in a difficult situation, wondering about what could possibly be the solution to our problem. Sometimes it seems as if we must become as brokenhearted and helpless as possible for salvation to come. The Tanya teaches us that even in troublesome times, one has to serve God with joy; many times, salvation will come about through our being in good spirits and feeling happy, rather than through a feeling of defeat. Often things work out better and faster if we pray to God from a place of joy and simcha, rather than from one of melancholy and self-defeat.

DANCING WITH THE FOOD

O NE DAY, when Reb Shmuel Munkes was attending a farbrengen, in walked the chef with a platter heaped with sweetbreads—a real delicacy. All the Chassidim were very pleased. Now, when they lifted their wine glasses to toast L'Chaim—*To life!*—they would have a delicious chaser to go with it.

Everyone knew that Shmuel Munkes could be a jokester, but even so, they were shocked when he jumped up, snatched the platter from the chef, and began dancing merrily around the room, holding the sweetbreads over his head like a performer showing off a prize.

The meat smelled delicious, and since all the Chassidim were feeling rather hungry, they began shouting at him, "Stop it! Don't do that! You're going to drop it, give it here! Let us eat it! Pass it over! Enough with your games!" But Shmuel Munkes just kept on dancing and prancing around the room, holding the platter up high, and no one could catch up to him.

All of a sudden, as he danced along the back of the room, Shmuel Munkes flipped the platter right over, and all the sweetbreads fell straight into the trough set in the floor, which was where the garbage was thrown back in those days.

By now the Chassidim were beside themselves with frustration and yelled even louder: "Why did you do that?! What were you thinking? Wasting food is a sin!"

As the Chassidim gathered around Shmuel Munkes, shouting in anger, the chef rushed into the room, his hands thrown up into the air, his face as white as a ghost. "No, no, no," he cried in an anguished voice. "Please, please, don't eat the sweetbreads! It's *treif*—it's not kosher!" The Chassidim were so shocked that they quieted down immediately. "By accident," the chef explained, "I switched the kosher meats with the non-kosher meats, and I gave the non-kosher meats to you. I am so sorry."

When the Chassidim told him about Shmuel Munkes's antics with the sweetbreads, the chef heaved a huge sigh of relief. "Thank God, the treif has been tossed into the trough!" he told them.

Now the Chassidim, as they tend to do at a farbrengen, became merry once again and began teasing Shmuel Munkes. "Oh, so now you're a hidden tzaddik, are you?" they asked him. "We see that you have *Ruach ha-Kodesh*, divine spirit, for how else would you have known that the meat wasn't kosher? Why else would you have thrown it in the garbage? Obviously, you're a hidden tzaddik."

Shmuel Munkes laughed right along with the Chassidim. But then, suddenly, he grew very serious. "I am no hidden tzaddik," he lamented. "However, when I was young man and I came for my first *yechidus*, my first private audience with the Rebbe, I decided then and there that if anything from the physical world would ever give me tremendous desire, *taivah*, no matter what it was, then I would abstain from it. My desire to taste the sweetmeats was so great, I kept my vow, and I could not partake of them, so I threw them all away."

TEACHING

In Chassidic teachings, there are two fundamental concepts: *iskafya*, which means holding oneself back, and *ishapcha*, which means transforming oneself. Whenever one has a tremendous desire or a strong temptation, the first thing one should practice—even if the thing one wants is something that is permitted—is iskafya, to hold oneself back from partaking of it.

But iskafya alone is not enough. Next, one must experience ishapcha, which requires transforming oneself into a state of not having any desire at all. Holding oneself back, restraining oneself, should always lead to transforming oneself entirely so that the desire no longer exists. If done correctly, abstinence can elevate the food as much as partaking of it.

On the one hand, we should enjoy the physical and elevate the spark of godliness that is found within all material things; but, on the other hand, iskafya and ishapcha must also be practiced. Elevating the spark of godliness within food to its source of holiness cannot be done by way of temptation or desire.

THE GREATEST SEDER

THE GREAT Reb Levi Yitzchak Berdichev was known as the great defender of the Jewish people. One year he had an especially wonderful Seder night. After the Seder, he sat marveling about how beautifully it had been conducted, and how he had been able to reach great spiritual heights. Eventually, he fell into a trance, and he heard a voice say, "So, you think you had such a great Seder? Well, Reb Shuelke the Water Carrier had a truly wonderful Seder, too."

The next morning, after services, he told his Chassidim, "Go get Shuelke the Water Carrier and bring him to me."

The Chassidim went to the home of Shuelke the Water Carrier, which was nothing but a little shed at the edge of town, and knocked on the door. When Shuelke's wife opened it she looked surprised, and then, hearing what they wanted, began to laugh. "You want my husband?" she said. "He's a drunk, good-for-nothing lowlife. He's been sleeping since last night."

The Chassidim persisted. They didn't easily take no for an answer when their rebbe asked for something. They ran right past Shuelke's wife into the bedroom, grabbed Shuelke off the bed and carried him all the way back to the Rebbe.

As Shuelke was coming back to himself, the Rebbe asked him, "Reb Shuelke, tell me, what did you do for the Seder last night?"

Reb Shuelke spoke humbly: "To tell you the truth, yesterday I realized that I wouldn't be able to drink whiskey for eight days, so in the morning I made sure to drink enough whiskey to cover that time. I got nice and tipsy. Afterwards, I took a nap. Sure enough, my wife kicked me a few times and woke me up, saying, 'Shuelke, let's go make a Seder.'

As I got up to make a Seder, my wife told me, 'You're a drunk. You're an ignoramus. You're a nothing.'

"So, you know what? I turned to my wife and I told her, 'You're right. I am an ignoramus. And I'm the son of an ignoramus. I don't even know how to make a Seder. But I know one thing: The Jewish people were slaves in Egypt, and God, our God, the God of our fathers, went and took us out of Egypt with great fanfare. And I know that right now we find ourselves in exile. We find ourselves in a tough situation. But I also know that, once again, God, this great God of ours, is going to redeem us from this exile as well.' I saw that my wife had put out wine, so I drank four cups of it. I saw that she had put out matzah, so I ate it—and I saw the eggs, so I ate them. Then, I was feeling tired, so I went back to bed."

Reb Levi Yitzchak turned to the Chassidim and said, "You see, when Reb Shuelke said that we find ourselves in exile and that God, the great God of our fathers, is going to redeem us again, he really meant it."

TEACHING

The Rebbe Menachem Mendel Schneerson, the Lubavitcher Rebbe, often mentioned in his talks that we all have the obligation to teach other people what we know, so even if all someone knows is the first letter in the Hebrew alphabet, the *aleph*, he still must teach someone else who does not know that letter. This is because, no matter how much or how little we know, we still have the power to teach and inspire others. This is because every single one of us is inherently connected to God. We do not need superior intellectual capacity, knowledge of the mystical worlds, or even a great knowledge of Torah, in order to approach and have a relationship with God. Having a relationship with God is a basic tenet of being human. God was involved in the creation of each one of us, so we are inherently and directly connected to him. Therefore, even if you acknowledge that you don't know that much, but you utilize that little bit of knowledge to connect to God—then whatever you know, even just the letter aleph, can bring about a tremendous power of connection to the Almighty.

The Substituted Matzah

ONE YEAR, on the morning of the first day of Passover, Reb Yehoshua Heschel of Apt, also known as the Apter Rov and the Ohev Yisrael, bundled up some matzah that had been prepared in a very special way for the Seder that night and placed them on the table near the door.

But then what happened? While the Rebbetzin was busy in the kitchen preparing the Passover feast, a poor person knocked on the door, asking for matzah for that night's Seder. A member of the Rebbe's household opened the door and, unaware that the bundle of matzah on the table was special, gave it away to the poor person.

A few moments later, the Rebbetzin stepped out of the kitchen, and when she saw what had just taken place, she totally panicked. At first, she didn't know what to do. But she was a smart person, so she quickly got some regular matzah, wrapped it up in the same special way and laid the bundle on the table by the door. That night, the Apter Rov conducted his Seder with the substituted matzah, as if nothing had happened.

Everything went on as normal for several weeks, until one day, a man walked into the Apter Rov's office, and announced, "Rebbe, I want to divorce my wife."

The Apter Rov was taken aback. "Why do you want to divorce your wife?"

The man said, "Because I hold higher standards of kashrut. And since my wife won't adhere to the laws of keeping kosher, I want a divorce."

The Rebbe stroked his long beard, listened to what the man had to say about his wife's not keeping kosher the way he wanted, and then told his shamash, "Go call in the Rebbetzin, my wife."

The Rebbetzin came in and Ohev Yisrael told her, "Why don't you tell me what happened with the matzah on the morning of the first day of Passover."

The Rebbetzin looked frightened, but the Apter Rov reassured her, "Don't worry. Tell it to him." So she told the entire story about how the special matzah had been given away to a poor man by mistake, so she had replaced it with regular matzah, wrapped up in a similar way, and placed on the table by the door.

"I made believe that the regular matzah had been sanctified in the same special way, and I did this in order to keep a peaceful home, to have *shalom bayit*," the Apter Rov told the man who wanted to divorce his wife for not keeping kosher. "Please don't worry. You can also be lax with some of your customs in order that you have a peaceful home as well."

TEACHING

In Jewish practice and prayer, the verse "Oseh Shalom" discusses God bringing peace into the world. What's very interesting about this practice is that it is customary to take three steps backwards before reciting this verse. After taking three steps backwards, we say the prayer and continue moving about, bowing to our right, then bowing to our left, and finally bowing forward. Out of all of our prayers, none of the others are accompanied by this very unusual movement.

My grandfather, Rabbi Jacob J. Hecht, of blessed memory, used to say that the reason we do this is because when it comes to achieving *shalom*, peace, first you have to remove yourself from the situation, so you take a few steps back. But to maintain proper peace, we must compromise by moving a little bit to the right, a little to the left, and doing whatever is needed in that situation. God can only dwell where there is peace between his children.

What has kept the Jewish people around as a nation over these thousands of years of exile, challenges, trials, and tribulations is not the synagogue, but rather, the Jewish family. Therefore, it is of greatest importance that one should strive to have a peaceful home, even if creating a home filled with peace, shalom, means sometimes putting aside one's own spiritual journey and personal connection to the Divine and compromising. It is worth it.

The Power of Religious Faith

THE SUKKAH GUEST

I N THE late 1800s, the Chassidic Jews in Europe saw America as the *triefah medina*, the non-kosher country. Why? Because the Chassidic emigrants who returned to Europe from America told stories about how different things were there. Due to societal pressures, it is told, many observant Jews felt they were not able to practice their religion freely in America the way they could in Europe. Immediately upon arriving in America, the story goes, even Chassidim of significant stature would shave off their beards, begin wearing Western-style clothing, and perhaps change their names. Often, they even became totally assimilated into American culture, abandoning their religion and culture.

Not surprisingly, many Chassidic masters prohibited their followers from emigrating to the triefah medina. That included the great master in Poland, Rebbe Yechezkel Shraga Halberstam of Sieniawa, commonly known as the Sieniawa Rebbe, who was the son of the famous Chassidic master, Reb Chaim of Sanz.

My family, the Hecht family, has a personal connection to the Sieniawa Rebbe. Even though the Rebbe did not generally allow his Chassidim to leave for America, he did make a few exceptions. One of those exceptions was Reb Hersch Melech Hecht, my great-great-grandfather, who came to America in about 1880 with the blessing of Reb Yechezkel of Sieniawa. Our family has remained true to Chassidic practices and observances, and we continue to withstand the challenges of social peer pressure six generations later.

The festival of Sukkot takes place in autumn, just after Yom Kippur. The holiday, which lasts for seven days, celebrates the miracles that God performed to protect the Jewish people as they wandered throughout the desert for forty years. Until our ancestors could finally enter into the Holy Land, God created "clouds of glory" to surround them in the desert, shielding them from its dangers. Ever since then, as described in the Torah in Leviticus 23:42–43, Jewish families have honored God's providence by building a "booth" or hut known as a sukkah in which to live together for a week, remembering God's kindnesses. There are many laws and rules that must be followed in a sukkah's construction and the choice of its location in order for it to be deemed kosher, fit for use. Most importantly, the sukkah's roof must be covered with *sechach*, raw vegetation—branches and vines and grasses and bamboo detached from their source.

My grandfather, Reb Hersch Melech Hecht, of blessed memory, often told a story about a very poor couple back in Europe—so poor that they couldn't afford a knife or a pair of scissors. One year, when it came time for Sukkot, the couple had no tools to carry with them into the woods to find the material for the roof of their sukkah. Instead, they cut down branches and vines by tearing at them with their bare hands, and then they cut the grasses they needed by biting them off at the roots with their bare teeth.

When the couple finished working, they had a great pile of material with which to cover their sukkah, but they also had bloody cuts and scratches all over their hands, and their mouths were sore and bleeding. They could have asked for charity, but their dedication to this mitzvah was so strong that they wouldn't consider charity.

On the first night of Sukkot, this couple sat down at the table in their sukkah to begin their meal. Since they had no food to enjoy, they decided simply to sit in the sukkah together, singing songs and enjoying the holiday. Soon a knock came at the door, and a man walked in to join their festivities.

"Listen, sir," they told the stranger, "we would love to have you as our guest, but we have no food to share, nothing at all. You are probably in need of a good holiday meal; why don't you try going across the road to the other sukkah? There's a nice family there who have been performing *hachnassat orchim*—the mitzvah of inviting guests. If you go to their sukkah, you're sure to have a good Yom Tov festive meal. We're sorry we have nothing to offer you."

"It's the first night of the holiday," the guest said. "You know about the *ushpizin*, the mysterious, otherworldly guest? Well, tonight, on the first night of Sukkot, I come to your table as the ushpizin. I am Abraham, your forefather."

The couple felt ashamed for not having any food to offer, but Abraham would have none of their apologies, and he refused to go to the "better" sukkah down the road.

"I have come to visit you," he insisted, "not because of whatever delicacies you may or may not have on your table, but because of the self-sacrifice you have shown by building your sukkah with your own bare hands, with no help whatsoever. I prefer to stay here with you and enjoy your fellowship rather than any meal."

⚜ TEACHING ⚜

One of the greatest mitzvahs is *hachnassat orchim*, inviting guests to our table. But too prevalent is the perspective that whoever we invite to dinner must be fit to sit at our table. We might think, "Oh, no, I can't invite Mr. So-and-So because he's not from my socioeconomic background." Or maybe: "It could never work for me to share a meal with those people because they don't agree with me politically or share my religious views, so what could we possibly talk about?" These are just some of the excuses we come up with for not inviting certain people to dine at our table.

But let's flip the coin, so to speak, and instead of deciding which guests are fit for us, ask ourselves: Am I fit to have this guest? Am I properly conducting myself to merit the honorable guest coming to my table?

The couple in this story couldn't invite any guests to dinner for Sukkot because they had no food to cook, nothing at all to offer. Yet the greatest of all guests, Abraham himself, showed up, completely astounding the couple. Despite there being no actual meal to be had, Abraham remained with them. He chose the couple for their strength of faith, purity of spirit, and commitment to the fulfillment of mitzvot, all of which he valued above shar-ing a delicious meal.

The tradition of hachnassat orchim dates back to Abraham, who set up a hotel in the form of a large tent along a well-traveled route, giving himself the opportunity to offer guests food, drink, and a place to sleep.

At the age of ninety-nine, Abraham received the commandment from God to circumcise himself, which he did. One day shortly thereafter, he lay sick in bed in his hotel on a boiling hot day. Despite being ill and uncomfortable, Abraham was bothered by the fact that he had no guests, until suddenly God paid him a visit. While they sat talking, God noticed that Abraham was in pain, so He sent three angels disguised as men to visit the hotel. When Abraham saw the three men outside, he turned to God and said, "Hey, God—hold on a minute. I need to attend to the men outside." He ran out of the tent and told the three men, "Please do not pass by this area; please stop as my guest so I can host you." From this story, our rabbis teach us that inviting guests into our home is even greater than communicating directly with God.

The Tutor, the Prince, and the Bagel

Y EAR AFTER year, on their annual visit to the Ba'al Shem Tov, a childless couple would ask him for a blessing to start a family—and year after year, the Ba'al Shem Tov refused to give them one, and they went home disappointed. Finally, one year, after much pleading from the couple, the Ba'al Shem Tov gave them a blessing for a special child.

Within a year, the couple was blessed with the birth of a baby boy, and they were filled with joy. Their child was a happy one until he was two or three years old, when suddenly he began to cry a lot and could not be consoled at all. The couple brought him to several doctors, but none of the experts could find anything medically wrong with him, so finally they took him to the Ba'al Shem Tov. "What can we possibly do to comfort him?" they asked.

"Give the child a bagel," the Ba'al Shem Tov answered. So that night, as instructed, the couple took the child home and fed him a bagel. At last the child calmed down again and fell asleep. But during the night, his sleeping soul returned to his Creator.

Heartbroken and beside themselves with grief, the couple returned to the holy Ba'al Shem Tov. "It was painful not to have a child, but it is even worse to have had a child and to have lost him," they cried bitterly.

"Let me tell you a story," the Ba'al Shem Tov said. "Once, in a distant land, there were a king and queen who had only one son, whom they loved dearly. They wanted to give the prince the best education possible so they searched throughout the land until at last they found a tutor of the greatest caliber and stature to teach their son every subject that was known at that time: reading, writing, mathematics, geography, astronomy. The tutor agreed to take the job under one condition: Every single day, for a two-hour period, he was not to be disturbed. So, every day at the appointed time the tutor would disappear into his study, lock the door behind him, and spend the next two hours in complete solitude and privacy.

"A few years went by. As the young prince got older, he grew more curious about the tutor's private time. 'What could the tutor be doing every day in seclusion for two hours?' he wondered. Finally, he decided to find out for himself. One day, the prince hid behind the curtain in the study prior to the tutor's arrival and watched, wide-eyed, from his hiding place as the tutor came in, closed the door behind himself and locked it, and pulled a cloth bag from a secret drawer. Out of the bag, the tutor drew what appeared to be a white tablecloth, which he wrapped around himself. Then he pulled out two black boxes with leather straps. He attached one to his arm and the other one to his head. Lastly, the tutor took out of the bag a book printed in strange, black letters in a language the prince had never encountered. Then the tutor settled into his chair and began reading the book, shuffling and swaying as he turned the pages. For two hours, he read in deep concentration, whispering and chanting quietly to himself.

"The prince thought this was all very strange, but he was so mesmerized by what the tutor was doing that he began hiding in the study and watching him every day. Months went by like this, until one day, the boy lost his balance in his hiding place and fell over with a bang.

"The tutor was astounded to find the young prince in his study. 'What is the meaning of this? What are you doing in here?' he demanded. 'Why are you spying on me? This is my private time.'

"The young prince could only ask questions. 'Please, tell me what it is you're doing every day,' he begged the tutor. 'I've been watching you for some time now.'

"At first, the tutor was reluctant to explain, but eventually he came to trust the prince enough to confide in him. 'Truth be told, I'm a Jew,' he said. 'I have a commandment to wear a *tallit* and put on this set of small, black leather boxes, these phylacteries called *tefillin*, which contain scrolls of parchment inscribed with verses from the Torah. And then I pray.'

"The young prince became even more curious about the tutor's practices and begged for daily lessons in theology and religion, which his tutor gave him.

"Initially, the tutor believed that the boy's interest stemmed only from an intellectual standpoint, but over time he could see that the young boy had a real affinity for what he was learning. After some more years passed, and the boy became a young man, he told the tutor he wanted to convert to Judaism. 'But that's impossible!' the tutor objected. 'If you convert to Judaism, the king and the queen, your loving parents, will be so angry they will have me put to death.'

"'All right then,' the prince said. 'Just teach me everything there is to know about Judaism—the laws, the stories, and the concepts.' So the tutor taught him all of the deep Jewish subjects and concepts from the Torah, the Talmud, and the commentaries. However, even though the tutor meant for this to satisfy the young prince's desire, it only made the boy even more curious.

"'I really want to convert, and I need you to help me,' the prince told his tutor a few years later. 'Here is what I'm going to do: I'll tell my parents that we have to go on a journey to study stargazing on the other side of the world. Once we've left the kingdom and are safely far away, I'm going to convert to Judaism.'

"And, in fact, that's what they did. They traveled to a distant land where the young prince converted to Judaism. He grew up to be a great Torah scholar and a leader within the local Jewish community. He lived a good, long life, and after he passed away his soul went up to Heaven. When his soul arrived, the supernal tribunal told him, 'Because you were a holy person and lived a good life, we'll send you straight to Paradise.'

"But the prince's soul objected. 'Knowing that I will receive my reward for doing good, I still have one desire. I want to be born as a Jew. Since I lived my life as a converted Jew, I now want to have the opportunity to be born from a holy union.'

"So it was decided that since he had been righteous on earth, he would be allowed to be born in a state of purity."

The Ba'al Shem Tov concluded his story, then turned to the couple and said, "You should be proud that you were the parents to bring this soul back into the world to be born as a Jew. You should feel honored."

 TEACHING

Whenever a soul comes into the world, we cannot know its purpose or its mission—sometimes a soul's mission is simply to be born. As difficult as it was for the couple in this story to lose their young child, they were able to understand that they had facilitated a pure and holy soul's coming into the world and fulfilling its mission.

Each soul, before it is born, abides in the glory and the splendor of God. When a soul is chosen to be born—that is, when a soul is given the mission of coming into a physical body—that soul doesn't want to leave. The soul says, "Life is great for me here. I don't want to end this." The soul knows that it must experience tremendous pain in order to come down into a physical body. In fact, the mother's own pains of labor, which she experiences in order to bring a new baby into the world, mimic the pain the soul goes through in making the descent from the spiritual abode into a physical body.

The reverse is also true. Once a soul is united with a body during life, that soul can see all that can be accomplished by being alive and by doing good. When it comes time to pass from this world, the soul that has performed physical mitzvot often does not want to be separated from its physical body. That is why, sometimes, when people pass away they experience prolonged illness and pain beforehand. Their physical suffering in death mimics the spiritual pain that their soul is experiencing in leaving its body. The soul realizes that in returning to the place of the spiritual, it will once again abide in the glory and splendor of God, but that it will no longer be capable of fulfilling God's commandments, performing mitzvot, and bringing God great joy.

Kosher Matzah for Passover in the Ukraine

The memoirs of Rebbetzin Chana Schneerson, the mother of the seventh Lubavitcher Rebbe, contain many stories about the hardships she endured with her husband, Reb Levi Yitzchak Schneerson, affectionately known as Reb Levik, when they were living in Yekatrinoslav, known today as Dnipropetrovsk, in the Ukraine.

The Rebbetzin tells how once, when the communist regime was trying to make a show of caring for the Jewish citizens in their region, some officials visited Reb Levik, who was chief rabbi, and asked him for a letter certifying that the wheat they planned to supply to the Jewish people to bake their matzahs for Passover was fully kosher according to his standards.

Reb Levik refused to certify the wheat as fully kosher unless he had proof that its growing and preparation actually upheld the standards of kashrut—and he told the regime that he would go to prison before he signed any claim that wasn't true. Surprisingly, the communist regime gave in and allowed him to supervise the growing and harvesting of the grain as well as the process of making it into flour so that the Jewish people of that region were able to have proper matzahs for the holiday of Passover.

 TEACHING

When Reb Levik refused to sign the kosher certification, he did not take into consideration the possible dire consequences for standing up against the communist regime for what is just and truthful. As Americans, we live in a place of freedom where we are not faced with such challenges. We should apply the same observances of the mitzvot with self-sacrifice and dedication. Being free does not mean being free of commandments; it means removing the yoke of man and replacing it with the yoke of Heaven. That's how a person reaches true freedom.

Jewish mysticism teaches that the martyrs willingly chose to die when faced with giving up their lives for the sanctity of God or converting to another religion. They did this because at that crucial moment of choice they experienced such a deep connection to God being awakened within themselves that they did not ever want to disconnect themselves from God, not even for a second. Instead, they chose to be disconnected from this life.

Martyrdom is the ultimate self-sacrifice. We may not all be called to be martyrs, but we all need to include self-sacrifice in our everyday lives. Each day, when we're faced with a challenge or a temptation, we can use the principle of self-sacrifice to make the right decision and avoid the temptation. We can choose never to lose our connection to God.

A L'Chaim to God

I N THE late 1700s, on the solemn eve of Yom Kippur, Reb Levik Yitz-chok of Berdichev, who was renowned as the defender of the Jewish people, stood in the synagogue, dressed in his white *kittel*, or robe, and his white tallit, or prayer shawl, solemnly poised to recite the *Kol Nidre*, the prayer to open the Day of Atonement. Reb Levik's face was radiant, as befitting such a righteous and holy person. But although everyone waited eagerly for him to begin speaking, he remained silent.

Five minutes went by, then ten minutes. As time passed, the people in the congregation began to whisper to each other: "What is happening? What could be keeping the saintly Rebbe from starting? What is he waiting for?"

Finally, when a poor man dressed in well-worn clothing sneaked in late and tried to hide in the back of the shul, Reb Levik began to speak. Pointing to the man, the Rebbe called out, "Come forward to me." The man, who was the local tailor, walked slowly to the front of the synagogue, looking humbly at the floor. "Tell me," the Rebbe asked when the tailor reached him, "what did you do today?"

The tailor looked nervous, but did not hesitate to answer. "To tell you the truth, Rebbe," he admitted, "I didn't feel the spirituality of the eve of Yom Kippur this year, so I decided to have a little drink. I made a little l'chaim to myself. After I drank my little l'chaim, I fell asleep. When I woke up, I realized it was only a few minutes before the holiday began. I also realized I hadn't eaten anything and I wouldn't even have time to prepare any food for myself to eat before the fast began. I only had time to pour myself another drink for a second l'chaim, so this time I made a l'chaim to God.

"'Ribbono Shel Olam, Master of the Universe,' I said to God, 'when I think about it, this past year, You weren't so nice. You left many women as widows, You left a lot of children orphaned, You left many people starving. Honestly, You didn't really do such a good job. On top of that, You're guilty of *lashon hara*, slanderous and evil talk, because if it wasn't for You, how would the local government have found out that I was cheating on my taxes?'

"Then I said to God, 'But I'll tell You what, in all honesty, I wasn't so good either this year. I could have studied more Torah, I could have done more mitzvot, I could have given more charity and helped more people. There were a lot of things I could've done better. So how about if I forgive You for that which You didn't do so well, and You forgive me for that which I didn't do so well? I'll make a resolution to do better this coming year, and You make a resolution to do the same. L'chaim!' And I drank my last drink and came to shul."

When the tailor finished his story, Reb Levik went to the podium and, with his face radiant, began to recite the Kol Nidre prayer. After the holiday ended, the Rebbe explained to his disciples that the tailor's confession and conversation came from a place of complete simplicity and sincerity, and that the tailor's l'chaim to God had caused an enormous, earthshattering amount of joyful commotion upon high for the Creator.

🕯️ TEACHING 🕯️

Our relationship to God must have many facets, including that of a parent to a child and a child to a parent. Just as a son loves his father, and as a father loves his son, so too must we approach our relationship to God. If we keep our commitments to God, God will keep his commitment to us. Sometimes it takes pure sincerity to truly fathom this relationship. Often, we are so impressed with our own intellect that we allow it to impede our sincerity and our sensitivity to God and weaken the relationship that we have with our God.

A Glutton for God

WE CALL Rabbi Israel ben Eliezer of Mezibu'sh "the Ba'al Shem Tov," which means "the Master of the Good Name," because he was able to take the ineffable name of God and use it to manipulate the physical world, circumventing limitations of time and space. He could use God's name to perform miracles, like healing the sick. And he could collapse time so that he could travel impossibly fast in his horse-drawn carriage to go and teach the people, or help them in some way, arriving after only one day at places that normally took three days or longer to reach. This is called *kefitzat haderech*, a shortening of the way.

One of the most important principles that the Ba'al Shem Tov emphasized was that there is a spark of God within the physical world and that it is humanity's role to elevate it. During the Ba'al Shem Tov's time on earth, Jews believed that becoming an ascetic, removing oneself from the physical world, was the most spiritual way they could live. People had such scorn and distaste for the physical world, especially their own bodies, that they would go out in the wintertime and roll in the snow, wanting to get cold and experience frostbite. And in the summertime they would lie down in the fields and let the ants bite them in order to torture themselves. The more people suffered in their bodies, the closer to God they felt. They believed that everything holy was spiritual, and that everything physical was unholy.

But the Ba'al Shem Tov taught that God is continuously creating the world anew, and that humans are comprised of two souls: a godly soul and an animalistic soul. It is our job to use the physical body to elevate the sparks we find throughout the world to their source in godliness. One of the ways this can be done, the Ba'al Shem Tov taught, is through food. When a person enjoys a meal properly—by eating kosher food, making a blessing before the meal and another blessing afterward, and using the food's energy to do good—that person can take the spark of God contained within the food and elevate it to a higher level.

The Ba'al Shem Tov wanted to find out who his companion would be in Heaven, and it was revealed to him from on high. He was told that in such-and-such a city, there was a man named Moshe, and that this person was going to be with him through all eternity. Of course, the Ba'al Shem Tov wanted to meet this Moshe, so he traveled to that city to look for him. When he arrived, he found that the people there were very excited about his visit. "The great Ba'al Shem Tov is here!" they all told one another, and they held a huge celebration and a procession through the city in his honor. But the Ba'al Shem Tov would not let anyone forget why he had come. "Listen," he kept telling everyone he met, "I'm looking for a man named Moshe."

"There's nobody in this city named Moshe," everyone said. But the Ba'al Shem Tov kept insisting, "I know he's here—I must find Moshe!" So the people searched high and low, until finally they found a man by the name of Moshe who was living on the outskirts of the city. But this Moshe was not what anyone was expecting. Moshe was a simpleton. He didn't even know how to read Hebrew. So the people said, "No, this can't be possible! The great Ba'al Shem Tov wants us to find this nobody, this insignificant being?!" They begged the Ba'al Shem Tov not to bother with Moshe, but in spite of their pleas, the Ba'al Shem Tov went to meet him anyway.

Now, aside from being simple, Moshe weighed four hundred pounds. He was massive, but completely unashamed of it. He spent the entirety of every day eating—that was actually the only thing he ever did.

When the Ba'al Shem Tov finally met Moshe, he thought, "I have to be with this guy for all of eternity? How can this be? There must have been some special mitzvah, some really good action that this person performed in his lifetime! There must be some secret as to why this man gets a special place in Heaven. There must be some good reason why I'm to be with him forever."

So he inquired of Moshe, "What do you do?"

And Moshe shrugged and replied, "I eat. I wake up in the morning and I eat all day."

"But what else do you do?" the Ba'al Shem Tov asked. "Surely there's something else."

Moshe shrugged. "I eat," he replied. "I wake up in the morning, and I eat all day long."

The Ba'al Shem Tov didn't know what to think of Moshe, so he sat there looking at him.

Finally, Moshe asked the Ba'al Shem Tov, "Do you know why I eat all day?"

"No," said the Ba'al Shem Tov. "Tell me."

"Well," Moshe said, "when I was a little child, six or seven years old, there was a pogrom, and they came into town and took my father away to burn him at the stake for being a Jew. My father was a scrawny, boney little individual, and while he was burning, I thought, 'If a Jew has to burn simply for being a Jew, then he is burning for God.' And I vowed, right then and there, that if they should ever come to take me and burn me at the stake for being a Jew, then I'm going to make sure I'm big enough to burn brightly and for a long time, the way a Jew would burn for God."

🕯️🕯️ TEACHING 🕯️🕯️

Moshe's whole existence was devoted to eating. Every day he indulged in food in what seemed to be the worst possible ways. He was obese and unhealthy. He was a complete glutton. How many steaks could one person eat?! Yet Moshe's motivation was such that he merited a place in eternity right next to the Ba'al Shem Tov, the greatest of all the Chassidic masters. For the simple yet sincere Moshe, who couldn't read Hebrew and didn't even know how to learn, every bite of food that he took was not for pleasure (although it may have tasted good) but for God. On the one hand, Moshe's eating was pure indulgence; on the other hand, it was a sacrifice, because he gave up everything else to do it. Eating was the greatest service to God that he could do.

Moshe ate for God so that if he were burned at the stake, he would become a *korbon*, a martyr. "If I have to be burned, then I want to show them what a Jew burning at the stake for the sake of God looks like," he said. Moshe served God with every bite he took and every pound he gained. The larger he became, the greater was his sacrifice for God.

Another person studying Torah or performing a mitzvah may not be as sincere or as devoted to God as Moshe was in his eating. Moshe found the spark of godliness in his food, and he spent his life elevating it. And we, too, may elevate physical things through indulgence.

The Choicest Pieces

T HE RAV of Volta, a Chassid of the Maggid of Mezeritch, was known for his tremendously deep understanding of both the Chassidic and the Kabbalistic concepts of Torah. But later on, during his life in Russia, the Rav began to drink, in order to calm his mind, until he became an alcoholic. Often, he went from *kretchma* to *kretchma*, inn to inn, getting drunk and passing out in front of the fireplace. Unfortunately, as the saying goes, *nichnas yayin yotzei sod*— when wine enters, the secrets come out—so when the Rav of Volta got drunk, not only was he no longer erudite, but he would also lose his sense of boundaries and just blabber to himself in public about deep Kabbalistic concepts.

However, until the end of his life, the Rav of Volta also said things that were so wise and true, they were startling to hear. Once, while traveling through the city of Liozna, the Rav came upon Reb Shneur Zalman of Liadi, who was then still known as the Maggid of Liozna. Reb Zalman, who later headed a branch of Chassidic Judaism, was in the middle of giving a Chassidic discourse. The Rav of Volta stood in the back of the room, listening closely. Afterward, as he walked out, he remarked, "We've all eaten from the same plate. But the best pieces, the Maggid of Liozna took."

 TEACHING

In this story, food consumption serves as a metaphor for how we take in what we are taught. Torah study has two parts. The first part is the Torah itself, which requires that one possesses a healthy level of ego to delve into the subjects at hand, and perhaps even come up with some innovations of one's own. The second part of Torah study is called the Word of God, which is the law, the decision. One must have total humility to study that part. At times, the actual decisive law may go against the very fiber of one's being, therefore requiring one's complete humility to accept it. During the times of our sages, there were great scholars who argued widely varying opinions. But when it came to the majority accepting one view, the person giving the second opinion needed to accept that view with humility.

BUT THIS MEAT ISN'T KOSHER!

O NCE THERE were two gentlemen who had known each other as children in White Russia and had both grown up in very religious homes. As adults they remained such good friends that they often traveled together for business. As their respective businesses grew more and more successful, they found themselves journeying far away, rubbing shoulders with many non-Jewish aristocrats in the upper echelons of society. As religious Jews, they felt a little uncomfortable in those situations, and because of that, over time they became lax with certain observances, such as the laws of kashrut and the way they dressed. One thing led to another, until they were finally assimilated into non-Jewish, aristocratic society and had abandoned all their former practices.

During one of their business trips, the two gentlemen were traveling through the White Russian forest when they came across a very charming cottage where a family of peasants lived. Since they were tired from having journeyed for many hours, they decided to stop. They knocked on the door and told the man who answered it, "We need to rest and to eat. Why don't you allow us to rest up here? And if you could please cook us a meal, we'll pay you handsomely for it."

"All right," the peasant agreed. "What would you like to eat?"

"Well," said the two gentlemen, rubbing their hands together in anticipation of a fine meal, "we would like a nice piece of meat, some vegetables, and some potatoes."

"But I don't understand," the peasant said. "You both appear to be Jewish; surely you must know that my meat isn't kosher."

The two gentlemen chuckled. "It doesn't matter that your meat isn't kosher," they assured the peasant. "We don't follow the laws of kashrut anymore—in fact, you can even add some milk to the meat if you'd like, if it will enhance the flavor."

"All right," said the peasant. "I'll be right back."

The peasant left the two gentlemen waiting for a few minutes. They expected him to reenter the room carrying some tea and bread, but instead he came in holding an axe in his hands, his face red with rage. "Gentlemen," he thundered, raising his axe high, "your time is up! I'm going to kill you both! I'm giving you an hour to prepare yourselves to be put to death!"

The two gentlemen were so stunned they could hardly speak. Finally, one of them, quivering, managed to ask the peasant, "But why?"

"It's very simple," the peasant said. "I rob people for a living. People stop here asking for food and rest, and every time they stop, I rob them, and then I kill them and bury them out back in the forest." And with that, he left the room and locked the door behind him.

The two gentlemen didn't know what to do. They knew there was no way out, and they could hear the man in the other room, sharpening his axe and telling his sons to go and dig fresh graves. The gentlemen were growing more and more terrified, and they trembled as they reminisced about their childhood together. In shaky voices, they regretted aloud doing the things that had led them to this very cottage, where they would now meet their deaths. "If only we had lived our lives differently, we wouldn't have found ourselves here, about to die," they lamented.

After an agonizing hour had passed, the peasant returned, grabbed each of the gentlemen by the throat, and dragged the two of them into the next room. Again, he left them alone, locking the door behind them, and shouting through the door, "Ten more minutes until I return to kill you both!"

Now the two gentlemen were overcome, not just with regret about the lives they had been living but also with tremendous remorse. They broke down and cried, falling to their knees and begging the Almighty to absolve them before they died. "Please forgive us for all our sins," they cried, over and over. "We are so sorry that we abandoned our religious observances. We have behaved poorly and shamefully." In that moment, they turned their backs completely on the depraved lives they had been living, and sincerely embraced their Jewish faith once again.

No sooner had they confessed then the door swung open once again. There stood the peasant, smiling amiably down at the two men, who still lay sobbing on the floor. "Come on out now," the peasant said in a kindly voice. The two weeping gentlemen struggled to stand; trembling hard, they stepped through the door as the peasant had commanded.

"You're free to go," the peasant told them calmly.

The two gentlemen nearly fainted. "What just happened?" one of the men asked. "We don't understand!" the other man said, nearly fainting.

"Let me tell you a story," said the peasant. "In 1776, a holy man was passing through this forest, and stopped here for a rest. He died in the room you were just in. But before he passed away, he blessed me with longevity, and he told me that if I ever came across two Jewish men who were irreligious and would happily eat food that isn't kosher, I should scare them until they repented."

The two gentlemen were very taken aback by this experience and asked the peasant who the holy man was. "He was Reb Shneur Zalman of Liadi, the famous founder of the Chabad Chassidic movement," the peasant answered. Then he led the two gentlemen to the master's gravesite nearby, where they prayed and committed to return to living as proper observant Jews.

TEACHING

The Torah provides a set of principles and laws that guide us through the day, from the very moment we wake up in the morning until we go to sleep at night. In Hebrew, the word "prohibited" is *assur* and the word "permitted" is *muttar*. The literal translation of assur is "tied or bound," and the translation of muttar is "untied or unbound." Prohibited food is not capable of being elevated because it is bound; food that is permitted can be elevated because it is not tied down.

Food is tremendously powerful, for it sustains our bodies as well as our hearts and minds. If we make sure that what we eat is properly kosher, food can guide us in the right direction. But if we do not eat kosher, what we eat will have the opposite effect, desensitizing us to spirituality, godliness, and all that is pure and holy.

The Chofetz Chaim and the Challah

THE FIRST food we eat at a traditional meal is bread, but on Friday night at our Shabbat meal, we begin with a cup of wine to sanctify the day. As we say the Kiddush blessing, we cover the loaves of challah with a cloth, so we don't hurt the bread's feelings for not beginning with it. After the Kiddush has been recited, and we've completed the washing of our hands, we uncover the challah and make a blessing over it. Then we start the Shabbat meal.

One Friday night, Rabbi Yisrael Meir Kagan, known as the Chofetz Chaim, visited a home where the woman of the house did not know all of the laws and customs surrounding the Shabbat dinner table. As the husband was about to make the Kiddush blessing, he realized that the challah loaves weren't covered and was angered by this. "The holy Chofetz Chaim is here!" the man shouted at his wife. "How is it possible that you should show your ignorance by not covering the challah?"

The Chofetz Chaim turned to the man and said, "The reason we cover the challah is to be sensitive to the loaves of bread because normally we begin our meal with bread, but on Shabbat, we start with the wine instead. How much more so does one have to be sensitive to another person's feelings and not make disparaging comments about them in public?"

 TEACHING

In *Pirkei Avot* (*Chapters of the Fathers*), we learn that even though someone follows all the commandments, if he embarrasses someone in public, he can lose his share in the world to come. This is very interesting: If you embarrass someone, you are not necessarily breaking a commandment that you could be punished for. For example, if you steal from someone, you must pay them back, plus a penalty, but there is no such punishment for embarrassing another person in public. And yet the damage that can be caused to someone by embarrassing them can be so profound that the person who commits such an act may suffer the greatest loss possible.

In this story, the Chofetz Chaim goes out of his way to make sure that he is sensitive to the woman because of his position in her presence. Due to the esteem which the husband and wife both accord him, the wife feels especially embarrassed in the situation. So when it comes to the precept of not embarrassing anyone, one must take into consideration both the act and the individual, with special sensitivity to the individual's feelings, which is something that is, unfortunately, often lacking today.

The Prodigy and the Butcher

WHEN THE great Reb Meir of Premishlan was a child, he advanced so quickly through the local school that his family had to find a private tutor to keep him stimulated. By studying hard, he amassed an amazing amount of knowledge even before he became an adult.

One day, as the young Meir was walking through the local marketplace, he ran into a butcher who had come to buy a cow to slaughter so he could sell the meat. By then, Meir was known for being an incredible *iluy*, a child prodigy. When the butcher saw this young boy, who was already famous for his ingenuity, he called him over to ask his opinion.

"I'll give you a ruble if you tell me which cow is kosher," the butcher said.

The boy wanted a better deal. "No," he told the butcher. "For one ruble, if you tell me which animal you're thinking of buying, I'll tell you if it's kosher or not."

"All right; how hard could this be?" the butcher said, and he handed Reb Meir a ruble and pointed to one of the cows. The boy looked the cow over carefully, and turned to the butcher and shook his head. "It's not kosher," he said.

"All right," said the butcher. "What about this one over here?"

"You've got to pay up first," Meir said. So the butcher gave him another ruble.

On and on this went, with the butcher paying Meir one ruble after another, until finally the boy said, "*That one* is kosher."

Why did the young Meir want the money? Even as a child, he was an entrepreneur and a generous sort. He ran a *fredaka*, a charity fund, to distribute money to the poor, so anytime he could make a little extra money, he took advantage of it so he could support his fund.

The butcher bought the cow that Meir had chosen, and sure enough, it was indeed kosher. The next day, the butcher went to the marketplace once again, found Meir, and paid him a ruble per cow until the boy pronounced one of the cows as kosher.

After a few weeks of this arrangement, the other butchers in town, who were all competitors, began talking about the butcher who was working with Meir. They said, "How is it possible that every animal this guy slaughters is perfectly kosher? He must be cheating; there's no way he's really selling all-kosher meat." This created a huge tumult in the town.

The butcher was outraged at being called a cheat. "It's not true," he insisted. In an effort to defend himself, he even told everyone about Meir, the boy genius whose help he had kept a secret until then.

News traveled quickly through the town, and one day the secret of Meir working with the butcher got back to the boy's tutor, who called Meir into his study. "Meir," the tutor said, "just because you're given a gift doesn't mean you have to use it." And from then on, Reb Meir gave up helping the butcher choose a kosher cow.

ᚐᚐᚐ TEACHING ᚐᚐᚐ

We're taught to believe that children lack a certain sensitivity to holiness, God, and spirituality—but actually, the opposite is true. Denying children proper education in these areas stifles their sensitivity. At a very young age, children are very perceptive. They have the capability to comprehend the spiritual and the willingness and sensitivity to embrace the reality of godliness, the realm of holiness. We have to allow them to participate in the holy, and we need to educate them to be involved, rather than stifle them. We must bring children up in a way that nurtures them spiritually.

By the same token, a teacher has an obligation to make sure their students conduct themselves in a befitting manner. The proper path is never to use your gift for personal gain. In this story, Meir didn't want the money for himself, nevertheless his tutor recognized that he needed to learn to earn the money by his own effort, without relying on any of his greater spiritual powers. God wants the world to conduct itself according to the natural order of things: If Meir wanted to earn money for his charity organization, he needed to go out and chop some wood to be able to earn a few dollars to use to run his organization to help people. It wasn't right for young Meir to use his gifts in a manipulative way. Although he was doing so for good reasons, it didn't make it right.

BUT IS THIS FOOD KOSHER?

R EB SIMCHA Bunim of Peshish Cha was once given a mission by his master, Reb Yaakov Yitzchak of Polonya, to travel to a certain village. Mysteriously though, his master didn't tell him the purpose of the trip. But since a good Chassid never questions his rebbe, Reb Simcha Bunim immediately began making plans to travel. After he got together a group of Chassidim to accompany him, he hired a wagon driver and they all went directly to the designated city to stay at a particular inn.

While traveling, the Chassidim's custom was to eat dairy products, for eating dairy is less complicated than eating meat when it comes to kosher dietary laws. With meat, it's necessary to know many intricate details regarding the slaughterer, such as whether he knows the kosher laws and is a God-fearing person, and that isn't always possible on the road.

Once they had checked in to the inn, Reb Simcha Bunim and his group headed straight to the dining facility to order some dairy food to satisfy their hunger. But the innkeeper told them, "In this facility, unfortunately, we have no dairy; we only provide meat." The Chassidim began interrogating the innkeeper about the status of the kosher meat, asking a host of relevant questions. "Who's the slaughterer?" they wanted to know. "What type of animal are you serving? How was it killed? How was it salted? Which Jewish and rabbinic authorities did the slaughterer follow?"

They went on and on with their questions until at last a man who was seated near the fireplace turned around and called out to them, "For all that goes into your mouth, you're so scrupulous, but are you as careful about what comes out of your mouth?"

Reb Simcha Bunim, an astute Chassid, understood that his master had sent him on this trip to hear what this man had just said, so he informed his fellow Chassidim who had traveled with him, "We can leave now—we have accomplished our mission." Immediately, Reb Simcha and his group of Chassidim checked out of the inn and got back into the wagon to travel home.

 TEACHING

Sometimes we aren't as careful as we need to be about what we're saying and how we're saying it. For instance, many parents tell their children, "Sticks and stones may break your bones, but words will never hurt you." That is actually the most dishonest thing we can teach our children. A broken bone can heal, but sometimes the comments people make are so callous and hurtful that we can never heal completely from their words. Words are more powerful and carry a far greater weight than any stick or stone.

Today, we are at least as strict about what we eat as Reb Simcha Bunim and the Chassidim were—and sometimes we go to great lengths to make sure our dietary needs are met. Many of us are on special diets, for instance: vegetarian or vegan, pescatarian, kosher, gluten-free, or paleo. Whatever kind of diet we choose to follow, we're cautious about what we eat. But are we always careful about how we express our needs when it comes to food? Like the stranger at the inn said, we need to be as mindful about what comes out of our mouths as we are about what goes into them.

Food Comes from Heaven

EVERY MORNING the Rebbe from Lublin sat down at his table after prayers and rang a little bell to notify his *shamash*, his attendant, that he was ready to eat breakfast. Immediately, the shamash brought him breakfast, and when the Rebbe said grace after the meal, he would always add, "God, thank you for giving me such a delicious breakfast." This went on, day in and day out, for many years until, finally, one day the shamash got fed up with the situation.

"Enough with this!" the shamash said to himself. "Every morning I prepare the food, and what does he say? 'Oh, thank you, God, for giving me breakfast.' But God doesn't give him breakfast, *I* do! Every day I prepare a beautiful breakfast for him, and every day I'm ready and waiting to bring it in to him as soon as he rings his bell. But does he ever thank me? No, he thanks God instead!"

So the shamash decided to teach the Rebbe a lesson. All that day he was grouchy and sullen, wondering how to do it, until he finally came up with a scheme. "I'll show him," he swore. "Tomorrow morning when he rings that bell, I am not bringing him any breakfast—not a single morsel! Let him understand that just ringing his bell and thanking God doesn't bring you a meal. *I* bring it! And he should acknowledge that and thank me as his shamash, as someone who's been taking care of his physical needs all this time."

The next morning, the shamash didn't prepare anything for the Rebbe's breakfast. Instead, he sat in the kitchen, waiting for the Rebbe to return from synagogue and ring his bell so that he could teach the Rebbe that it was he, not God, who was responsible for feeding him.

Meanwhile, the Rebbe was sitting in synagogue, saying his morning prayers, when suddenly a man came in, very excited, and interrupted him. "Rebbe! Rebbe!" the man said. "My wife is in labor! Please pray for her that it's an easy labor."

"Of course, I will pray for your wife," the Rebbe said.

The man thanked him and rushed back to his wife.

After finishing his prayers, the Rebbe went home and sat down at his table as usual and rang the little bell. "Aha!" the shamash said to himself in the kitchen when he heard the bell. But he didn't move. He stayed put in his chair, grinning to himself, and folded his arms across his chest. "Let's see how the Rebbe likes *this*," the shamash thought. "I wonder how hungry he is, and how he'll react to going without any food."

But the shamash never found out. At that very moment, the Rebbe's front door was flung open. When the shamash went to see what the commotion was all about, he found a man standing there, holding a huge platter of delicacies. "Rebbe, Rebbe!" the man called out, striding past the shamash into the Rebbe's study. "My wife just gave birth and the baby is healthy! Thank you for your prayers. Here, I've brought you some breakfast."

Needless to say, the Rebbe's shamash learned a great lesson in humility that day.

 TEACHING

In this story, the shamash's ego got the best of him. He really felt that without him the Rebbe could not survive. But God showed him: "Hey, shamash, you think that you're in control, but that's not so. It's true that you participate in the Rebbe's daily life, but not everything in the Rebbe's life comes from you. You're a messenger making things happen, but you're not the one who causes things to happen."

Jewish mysticism teaches that Isaac had twin sons: Jacob, who represents that which is good and holy, and Esau, who represents that which is bad and unholy. Within ourselves, we each experience some ambivalence. Part of us identifies with Jacob, and another part identifies with Esau. The story of these two brothers demonstrates the two different reactions we can have when something good happens to us. We can have an unholy reaction like Esau, who became egotistical and selfish when he experienced good fortune, or we can react like Jacob, who experienced *katonti*, which means, "I have become small." When we experience katonti we are humbled by the good that happens to us. Jacob saw that God had bestowed upon him great mercy and goodness, and he was humbled by the special attention God had paid to him. Thus, the good that was bestowed upon Jacob actually instilled within him a greater level of humility and gratitude.

Maybe the most important teaching in the study of Chassidut is the importance of the trait of humility. Our negative ego creates a constant struggle within ourselves, so we must work to build a healthy, spiritual self-esteem that does not allow us to attach ourselves to many natural reactions such as anger and jealousy.

The Untouched Whiskey Distillery

REB CHAIM Elazar Spira was one of the greatest rebbes in the Munkacz dynasty as well as the author of a great halachic work, the *Minchas Elazar*, which discusses and defends many Chassidic customs from the perspective of Jewish law. He liked to tell this story about a Chassid who owned a whiskey distillery:

Once there was a Chassid who had a great life thanks to his thriving business. Each year, during Passover, because of the prohibition against owning any leavened bread products, he sold all of the whiskey in stock at his distillery to local non-Jews and leased his business to them as well. After Passover, he bought the whiskey and his business back.

The preacher at the local church was a real anti-Semite, and wanted to hurt the Jewish community. One year he told all of the non-Jews in the town that no one was allowed to lease the factory during Passover or buy the factory's whiskey. The preacher knew that an observant Jew would not violate the prohibition of owning leavened products on Passover, and he hoped to leave the distillery without an owner—which is exactly what happened.

That year, the Chassid went around town, looking for people to buy his whiskey and searching for someone to temporarily lease his business. Nobody wanted to do business with him. When the day before Passover arrived, the Chassid had no choice but to open up his prayer book and make the declaration that he did not own the distillery and all of the whiskey within it, just as the dust of the earth is ownerless, and he closed the door to his business and walked away.

The next morning, the anti-Semitic preacher told everybody, "Now that the distillery is ownerless, go up there and take as much whiskey as you'd like. Help yourselves!"

After Passover, on his way up to see the damage that took place to his distillery, the Chassid ran into a non-Jewish man he knew, and the man said, "I don't understand you. You declared that the place is ownerless, yet you stationed a watchman with a fiery sword in front of your distillery!"

"What?!" exclaimed the Chassid. "I did no such thing! I don't know what you're talking about!"

When the Chassid reached the distillery, he saw that not one casket or keg or barrel of whiskey had been touched. Everything was exactly as he had left it, untouched.

The Rebbe Elazar of Munkacz used to say that because the Chassid was so sincere in giving up all of his leavened products, God made it appear as though a watchman with a fiery sword was standing in front of his distillery protecting it.

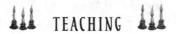

TEACHING

We all know and practice many commandments. But sometimes we practice these commandments simply out of habit, and we lack the sincerity to practice a commandment in the best possible way. If we perform a commandment with the greatest level of sincerity, doing it in the best possible way, then we can achieve such a high level of connection and draw down such a level of godliness that our performance can have an actual effect on the physical world—even to the extent of creating a watchman with a fiery sword to protect our physical assets.

MITZVOT!

THE BREAD IN THE ARK

THERE ONCE was a simple family who had learned about the historic mitzvah of the *Lechem Hapanim*, commonly known as the Show Bread. In ancient times, the Temple featured a table on which a dozen loaves of bread always sat. The Temple's *kohanim*, priests, would bake twelve new loaves of bread each week, and every Shabbat they would replace the loaves on the table with fresh ones and eat the old ones from the past week. The bread the kohanim baked was miraculous because, even though it sat out on the table for an entire week from Shabbat to Shabbat, it never went stale. The Show Bread was only one of the many daily miracles that took place in the temple.

After learning about the Show Bread, the family decided to fulfill it, so the wife baked twelve small loaves of challah, and right away the husband took them, still warm and fragrant from the oven, to the synagogue. There, he opened up the *aron kodesh*, the holy ark, where the Torah scrolls are kept, and announced, "God, I want to give you a gift. Lechem Hapanim!" Then he placed the loaves of challah inside, closed the ark's doors, and left.

A few minutes later, a beggar walked into the synagogue. He was so broken down by the hardships of his life that he approached the ark and cried out to God, "I have children at home, and they are hungry!" Just as he concluded his prayer, he suddenly realized he was smelling warm bread. "That's strange," he thought. "Where could it be?" He began walking around the synagogue, sniffing the air, but he could not tell where the delicious aroma was coming from until he was standing in front of the ark. Mystified, he opened it up, and was amazed to find inside the basket of twelve loaves of challah. "God has answered my prayers!" he cried. "I can't believe it!" With tears of joy streaming down his face, the beggar took the basket of bread home to feed his family.

The next day, the man who had fulfilled the mitzvah of the Show Bread returned to the synagogue for services. When the ark was opened and there were no loaves of bread to be seen, he was amazed. As soon as the services ended, he rushed home and told his wife, "God ate the bread!" Together, he and his wife began to dance with joy.

This happened week after week: The wife baked a dozen loaves of challah, and while they were still warm, her husband fulfilled the mitzvah of the Show Bread by taking the basket of fresh loaves to the synagogue and leaving them in the ark. And every week, the beggar would arrive soon after the man left to receive what he believed was a miracle.

Then, one Friday, the rabbi happened to walk in to see the beggar crying to God for food and opening up the ark. The rabbi was very surprised to see a basket of twelve loaves of challah inside. *"What's going on here?"* he wondered. So the very next Friday, the rabbi found a hiding place for himself in the synagogue so he could watch and find out what was taking place. Sure enough, in came the man with a basket of fresh bread. He stood before the ark, telling God he wanted to give him a gift, the Show Bread, and then opened up the ark and placed the bread inside.

As the man closed the ark and turned to leave, the rabbi jumped out of his hiding place and shouted at him, "It's despicable what you're doing, putting food in the ark!" The man was in shock. "But God eats the bread every week!" he cried.

"No, you fool, God doesn't eat the bread!" the rabbi shouted, and he explained what had been taking place. The rabbi admonished the man so severely for placing bread in the ark for the beggar that the man went home completely brokenhearted. "We can no longer perform this mitzvah because the rabbi won't allow it," he told his wife. "What fools we were to think God ate our bread."

A few days later, the rabbi received a visit from the Arizal, Rabbi Isaac Luria, who informed him that because he had told off the man for bringing bread every week, he was destined to die. The gift of the bread had been very enjoyable to Heaven, the Arizal explained. Since the destruction of the Second Temple, the mitzvah of the Show Bread had not been fulfilled until this man began making his gift. "Then, thanks to this man and his wife, the Lechem Hapanim began to be fulfilled once again every week," said the Arizal, "but then you put a stop to it." Of course, the rabbi broke down in tears and asked the Arizal for teshuvah, a method of repentance.

 TEACHING

We have been given many commandments that can't necessarily be fulfilled today due to the circumstances of exile or lifestyle restrictions. Nevertheless, we may be able to fulfill those mitzvot on a spiritual level, so it is worth searching for ways to do that. Sometimes we can fulfill an ancient mitzvah simply through studying it, as God will consider our coming to understand the mitzvah to be as if we had performed it; we can also perform an ancient mitzvah in a different way or on a different level instead of the way it was traditionally performed.

THE HOLY DRUNK

ONCE, ON the eve of Yom Kippur back in the eighteenth century, in the city of Berditchev in what is now Eastern Europe—a Chassidic man discovered that the local land squire, or *poritz*, had taken the innkeeper, who was also a Chassidic Jew, to court for falling behind on his rent—and the innkeeper and his family had been thrown into debtors' prison. So on the eve of the Day of Atonement, the holiest day of the year in all of Judaism, the poor innkeeper was suffering in the jail cellar, along with his wife and children.

The kind-spirited Chassid wanted to set free the innkeeper and his family, so he decided to raise the funds to pay the three hundred rubles in ransom money, which is what the innkeeper owed in back rent to the poritz. It was a huge sum of money to raise so quickly, but the Chassid knew it was the right thing to do. So, all morning long he walked up and down the streets of Berditchev, asking everyone he saw for a contribution. Since most people were preoccupied with preparing for the upcoming holiday, he didn't have much success, and after many hours of soliciting donations with no results, the Chassid was despairing. Then he remembered an elegant tavern which many nonobservant—or perhaps not yet observant—Jews frequented. "I've got nothing to lose," he thought. "I might as well go there and see if I can raise some money from these irreligious, aristocratic Jews. At least they'll have a few spare rubles to give away."

When the Chassid entered the tavern, the patrons were all surprised to see him there, and they grew quiet, staring at his *kapoteh*, his long, black coat, and his beard and *payos*, side curls. Then one man, who was drinking with a group of friends, stood up and announced to the crowd, "On the day before Yom Kippur, a Chassidic Jew walks into a bar! What could be his story?" Everyone laughed. Then the drinking man called the Chassid over to sit next to him at the bar.

"So, sir," the man asked as the Chassid sat down, "what brings you here?"

"It's very simple," the Chassid answered. "I'm here for a family that was thrown into debtors' prison. I'm trying to raise three hundred rubles so I can free them before tonight, in time for the solemn holiday of Yom Kippur."

The drinking man decided to have some fun with the Chassid so he could amuse his friends. "You know what," he boasted loudly, "I'll make a deal with you. I'll give you a hundred rubles if you drink a full cup of Zexun Nine Zeke—ninety-six proof vodka, which is the strongest alcohol available for consumption. That'll give you a third of the amount of the money you have to raise. But you've got to drink it bottoms-up or I won't pay you."

The Chassid considered the man's offer for a moment. On the one hand, he thought to himself, it was the eve of Yom Kippur, and if he drank Zexun Nine Zeke, he would have a hangover for the holy day. Plus, he would have more to atone for! But, on the other hand, if he drank the vodka, he would instantly have a third of the amount of money that he needed to free the family. In an instant, he would be closer to his goal. "It's a deal!" the Chassid shouted out.

The bartender poured a big, overflowing cup of Zexun Nine Zeke, and the Chassid sat up straight, squared his shoulders, and downed it in one go. Truth be told, it made him feel a little queasy, but now he had a hundred rubles in his hand, so he was happy. Meanwhile, all the people in the bar were going wild, laughing and shouting and toasting him. They thought he was the funniest thing they'd ever seen—a Chassid, dressed in a long, black coat, getting drunk in a bar on the eve of Yom Kippur. What entertainment!

"You know what?" said another man in the crowd. "I'll give you another hundred rubles if you drink a second cup." The Chassid agreed right away, so the bartender poured another cup of Zexun Nine Zeke. Again, the Chassid drank it straight down. This time he felt so sick that he moaned, and his head spun so badly that he held it in his hands, which only made the crowd laugh harder. "Oh, where am I?" he thought. "What have I done?" He was so drunk he could no longer tell whether he was sitting down or standing up, or whether he was still in the bar or outside on the street. "I'm finished!" he thought to himself.

But a third man emerged from the ruckus and told the Chassid, "I'll give you another hundred rubles, the final third of the money that you seek, if you drink just one more cup." The Chassid could barely see the man standing before him and holding out the final hundred rubles. Nonetheless, he gathered his wits about him and told the man, "You know what? If I can get the whole sum to free the innkeeper and his family, it's worth it—but I'll only do it if you agree to take me to the poritz to pay their ransom and then drop me off at shul." The man agreed, and as the crowd stomped and clapped and screamed with laughter, the Chassid downed the third cup of Zexun Nine Zeke and collapsed onto the bar.

The three men who had made bets with the Chassid kept their side of the deal. They accompanied him to the poritz, paid the ransom, and saw the family freed. Then they delivered the Chassid safely to the synagogue and plopped him down on a back bench, where he stretched out and promptly fell asleep.

Night turned to morning and the congregation began to arrive, all ready to observe Yom Kippur. Everyone was dressed in white robes, *kittels*, and prayer shawls, *talaysim*, and the Torah scrolls were removed from the Ark. As the synagogue filled up, people pushed the sleeping Chassid over to make room, and he woke up, still drunk. When he saw that the Torah scrolls were out of the Ark, he got confused about which holiday it was, for the scrolls are only removed from the Ark twice a year, first at Yom Kippur and again a few weeks later at Simchat Torah, which celebrates the conclusion of the annual cycle of public Torah readings and begins a new cycle.

Because he was still drunk, the Chassid thought it was Simchat Torah, and therefore a joyous holiday, not solemn Yom Kippur, so he jumped up on the bench and shouted, "*Ad kahn hakafa dalid*—here ends the fourth time of the circle dance around the Torah!" The congregation was horrified, and everyone shouted to the Rebbe, "Look at this lowlife! Look at this disgraceful drunk! Throw him out!"

But the Rebbe turned to the congregation and said, "No, no, he can stay here. We need him in our shul. He performed a mitzvah earlier today of redeeming captives, paying the ransom to free a family from debtors' prison. Because of this mitzvah, he was able to skip the spiritual journey of the holiday of Yom Kippur and go directly to the level of the holiday of Simchat Torah, which is on an even higher spiritual realm. I won't throw him out. He can celebrate while we all atone."

TEACHING

This story brings a question to mind: Why, on the eve of Yom Kippur, does it take so long for this Chassid to raise the funds to save a captive family? It seems like it should be quite easy for him to raise the funds, since on that day everyone is thinking about atonement and forgiveness and is more than ever aware of the importance of charity. So why is it that when the Chassid sets out to collect the money, he can't even raise a nickel?

The answer to this question has two parts. First, according to Jewish mysticism, we should contemplate the fact that this Chassid was given a specific challenge—to redeem the captive family—and that he took this mitzvah upon himself with great sincerity. God made the challenge as great as it could be in order to bring out the Chassid's greatest potential. By fulfilling this mitzvah, the Chassid would be able to reach the greatest spiritual heights and to delight in achieving holiness.

But there is another even more important reason that God did not allow the Chassid to raise the funds through the first people he met. If those people had donated money toward freeing the family, he would not have been able to present the aristocrats in the bar with a chance to fulfill a very special mitzvah. Even though the aristocrats were not observant, they also deserved a chance to do good. So the Chassid's difficulties raising the funds helped the aristocrats too.

The greatest mitzvah of all is the kind that one performs with total self-sacrifice for another person. In this story, the Chassid sacrificed his own spiritual journey on the eve of Yom Kippur to help the innkeeper and his family. Because of this, he was able to transcend the holiday's solemnity and advance straight to the higher spiritual plane of Simchat Torah. If we are willing to give of ourselves to help another person in the physical sense, we can transcend the normal chain of events in spiritual realms.

The Hungry Neighbor

WHEN I was a rabbinical student, I had the honor and pleasure of spending a year in Sao Paolo, Brazil, and studying at the yeshiva there. One of the *mashpi'im*, leaders, of the community was Reb Mottel Zajac, OBM, and I had the privilege of living for a month with him and his wife, Morah Rivkah.

When Morah Rivkah was growing up in the 1930s in communist Russia, starvation was common, and it was normal to feel hungry constantly. One day, her father was so desperate to feed his family that he traded a fur coat for a single loaf of bread. It had been many, many months, if not years, since the family had seen an entire loaf of bread, and there it sat on the table, a thing of wonder. All day Morah Rivkah looked at it, anticipating how wonderful it would taste that night for dinner.

That afternoon, a neighbor stopped by to speak with her father about a local matter. When the neighbor came inside, he noticed the loaf of bread on the table, and he too began staring at it. Out of politeness, Morah Rivkah's father offered the neighbor a knife and told him, "Please, help yourself." The man eagerly sliced off a piece of bread and ate it as they talked. Then he sliced another piece of bread, and ate it, followed by another and another and still another slice—until, finally, the entire loaf of bread was gone.

Morah Rivkah remembered seeing her siblings' eyes about to pop out of their heads as they watched this man eat all the bread and feeling her own hunger gnawing away even harder inside her. But all the children understood that the neighbor could not control himself because he, too, was starving—so not one of them made a sound.

🕎 TEACHING 🕎

This story made a great impression on me as a young adult. Here was a starving family who had made a huge sacrifice to score a single loaf of bread. Yet even as the children watched that bread being taken away from them, they had *kavod habriyot* —they were able to honor God by honoring others. Those children understood that their starving neighbor was, like them, a being created by God and therefore deserving to be treated with dignity. The children in this story showed incredible self-restraint and respect. They understood their neighbor's plight and, God forbid, would never say anything to embarrass him.

FEEDING THE POOR

O N THE day after Rebbe Akiva's daughter's wedding, his daughter came to him and told him the following story:

"When I arrived at the hotel after the wedding ceremony, the first thing I did was to stand in front of the mirror and remove the pins from my hair. I put the pins in a small hole in the wall that was designed to hold them.

"The next morning, when I woke up and took the pins out of the hole in the wall so I could put my hair up again, I noticed that there was a dead poisonous snake in the wall, and my pins had actually punctured its head and killed it."

Rebbe Akiva told his daughter that, in truth, it had been decreed in Heaven that she should pass away on her wedding night after entering the marriage canopy. But because she had performed a special mitzvah before her wedding, her life had been spared.

"What was the special mitzvah you did?" Rebbe Akiva asked her. "How did you occupy yourself on the morning of your wedding day?"

"Yesterday morning I woke up and went to the kitchen," his daughter answered. "I worked hard to prepare a beautiful meal. Then I packed the food up and carried it with me out into the streets. I went to find where all the beggars were and I fed them this meal. Knowing that my wedding day would be the happiest day of my life, that I would enter beneath the marriage canopy and begin my life anew, I felt I had to share my joy by giving to the downtrodden and taking care of the poor."

Rebbe Akiva explained to his daughter that because of this *zchut*, this merit, her life had been saved.

♨ TEACHING ♨

When we think about charity, we tend to think of great philanthropists. By the stroke of their pens they can write a check for a sum of seven or eight, or even nine, figures and they have the means to build grand buildings with their names across the front. In comparison, someone who spends their time simply cooking a meal for the poor seems to be less generous. However, from God's point of view, someone who puts in whatever energy and time he or she can to help another person is just as precious—sometimes even more precious—than the philanthropist's huge financial gifts.

It's often greater to give someone help that is less dramatic and showy but more immediate. There's a story recorded in the Talmud about this. Once there was a great rabbi, a sage, who was asked by a poor person for food. The rabbi gave the beggar money, but the man was so close to starvation that before he could go buy himself food, he passed away. The sage was punished. Why wasn't his deed considered charity in the spiritual realms? Because he should have given the beggar immediate help rather than money. He should have noticed how close to death from starvation the man was, and immediately gotten him some food to revive him.

When Fasting Is Not Holy

IN THE town of Apt, there was a very wealthy, pious man who felt that since he had already reached every level of spiritual service there was to reach, he should begin fasting one day a week. Before long, it didn't feel like one day of fasting was enough, so he started fasting two days a week. But that didn't seem like enough either, so he began fasting three days a week, and so on, until finally he was fasting all week long, from Shabbat to Shabbat.

After doing this for a few months, one Shabbat afternoon, right before the final meal, the man told his wife, "I think I'm going to go up the block to the church and convert to Christianity." His wife had never heard anything so crazy come from his mouth before. "That's not funny; stop making jokes!" she said. "Eat your hearty meal and get ready for your week of fasting."

So the man finished his final Shabbat meal, and the week passed as usual. But on the afternoon of the following Shabbat, as he sat down for his final meal, he told his wife once again, "I think I'll go to that church nearby and convert." This time his wife grew more concerned. "Eat, please eat," she coaxed him. "No more talking! Just eat and get ready for your week of fasting." Fortunately, she was able to convince him to eat; afterwards, she called their sons together and told them what had transpired over the past two weeks. They, too, were concerned and agreed to keep a close eye on their father.

Once again, the week went by as usual with the man fasting until Shabbat. But this time, no sooner had he sat down at the table for dinner than he stood up again, took off his *kippa* and tossed it to the floor, and then threw off his *bekishe*, his long black coat. "Excuse me now," he announced to his wife, "I'm going to walk up to the church and convert."

His wife rushed from the room and called for her sons to come quickly, and together they chased the man up the street. The sons caught up with their father as he was about to walk up the church steps and dragged him back home, where his wife tied him to the bed.

Thankfully, when the Shabbat ended, the man came to himself once again. But this time, his wife and sons took him to see Rabbi Avraham Yehoshua Heshel, known as Ohev Israel, or the Apter Rov. After they recounted the story of the man's repeated attempts to convert to Christianity, the Rebbe looked the man over and told them: "Take him home, tie him to the bed again, and for the next twenty-four hours, do not feed him any food. He's going to go totally crazy and beg you for drink or for food, but you have to stand strong. Don't give him anything. After twenty-four hours, feed him a full meal and don't let him start fasting. He has to eat every single day."

The family did exactly that. For twenty-four hours, the man alternately cried, screamed, and demanded water and food. "Please, I need something to drink. I'm thirsty. Just one drop!" he begged. "I'm hungry. I need to eat—just one morsel!" But the family held strong and did not give him anything to drink or eat for the entire twenty-four hours. When the time was up, they untied him and led him downstairs for a big meal, as the Apter Rov had advised them. The man ate happily and never tried to fast again, and life went back to normal.

Once everything had fallen back into place and the man was feeling like his old self again, he returned to visit the Apter Rov to ask him about what had happened. "You should know that food has two components," the Rebbe explained to him. "It brings physical nourishment, which is its material aspect. But food also brings spiritual nourishment. These two elements give a person both the physical and the spiritual strength to continue to do their work.

"When someone fasts *for the sake of God*, they're able to reach the concept of spiritual nourishment. When someone fasts *not* for the sake of God, but for himself, as you did, then they not only deprive themselves of physical sustenance but even worse, deprive themselves of spiritual sustenance as well.

"Every time you fasted, you actually gave energy to your evil inclination, your *yetzer hara*," the Apter Rov said. "Do you know why I made you fast one last time, for one more day? Because by performing the fast properly, for the sake of God, you were able to elevate all of the prior fasts as well."

TEACHING

In the *Tanya* (a book by Rabbi Shneur Zalman of Liadi, the founder of Chabad, defining Chassidic mystical psychology and theology) we learn that if one performs a mitzvah without *kavanah*, proper intentions, many times over, the mitzvah does not get elevated to lofty spiritual levels. However, if one performs a mitzvah just once but performs that mitzvah with proper kavanah, one has the power to elevate each and every time that one has performed that particular mitzvah in the past. For example, let's say someone prays every single day but does so without proper intention in an automatic, robotic way. If just once that person prays with proper intent and excitement and energy, that one time will elevate all those prior times of praying robotically and lacking soul.

Although kavanah is not required in the actual performance of a mitzvah, if a mitzvah is accompanied by kavanah, then that mitzvah soars to a greater height. According to Chassidut, a mitzvah accompanied with love and awe of God is like a bird: It can fly up high. But a mitzvah performed without the love and awe of God is like a bird without wings: It may be alive, but it cannot fly.

The Loan That Led to Spiritual Delight

ONE DAY, the Tzemach Tzedek of Lubavitch, Rabbi Menachem Mendel, who was the third Chabbad Rebbe, was on his way to shul for morning prayers when he bumped into a poor man. "Please lend me a few rubles," the poor man begged, "so I can go to the marketplace and buy some things, and later resell them at a profit. When I sell them I'll pay you back. I need to earn some money today so I can bring my wife some food so she can make dinner for our family tonight."

The Tzemach Tzedek, whose name means "plant" and "righteous person," was happy to help the poor man out. "Sure," he told him. "I'm happy to lend it to you. I'm on my way to shul, so come see me after I pray, and I'll give you a loan."

But when the Tzemach Tzedek arrived at shul and put on his tallit (prayer shawl) he realized something. "Wait a minute," he thought. "If I wait until after prayers to give that poor man a loan, he's not going to be able to go to the marketplace until later. And if he arrives at the marketplace late, he'll miss out on all the good deals. And if he misses out on all the good deals, he won't make any money. And if he doesn't make any money, he's not going to be able to put food on his table tonight, and his family will go hungry."

So the Tzemach Tzekek removed his tallit and hurried back out onto the street. He found the poor man right away and took him back to his house; in good faith he gave him a loan right away so that the man could go to the marketplace without delay.

Afterwards, the Tzemach Tzedek returned to shul to pray. As he was putting his tallit back on, he had a vision of his grandfather, Reb Shneur Zalman of Liadi, standing before him and looking at him with a big smile. It had been a very long time since he had seen a vision of his grandfather, and he knew that his grandfather had chosen to appear to him because he was pleased that the Tzemach Tzedek had done the poor man a favor.

TEACHING

In this story, the Tzemach Tzedek makes a poor man's interests his own. This is what God wants us to do. If you want to be a good parent, you should make the interests of your child your own. For example, if a child is interested in a certain style of music, then you should take interest in music as well, in order to be able to share it with your child and deepen your relationship. It's the same when dating: If there's someone you want to go out with, make that person's interests your own, and you will have a means of connecting with each other.

So it is with God. Love the people around you. Become interested in them. God loves these people, for they are his children, and He is interested in them. If you love these people too, then you're loving that which God loves and making the love of God your own love, thereby giving yourself a deeper relationship and connection to God. In fact, in the *Hayom Yom*, an anthology of Chassidic aphorisms and customs written and compiled by the Lubavitchter Rebbe, the Ba'al Shem Tov asks, "Which is greater: the love of our fellow man or the love of God?" The love of mankind is far greater, for by loving your neighbor you are actually loving what God loves.

The Vinegar-Flavored Cholent

IN THE old days, if a great visitor was coming to a certain city, the congregation of that city's synagogue would hold a lottery to determine who would host the visitor for the holy Sabbath. It was felt that it wouldn't be fair for the famous masters to stay only at the homes of the rich and famous. Everyone deserved a chance to host.

So one Friday, Rebbe Avigdor Halberstam, who was the brother of the Chassidic master Reb Chaim Halberstam of Sanz and was a great scholar and a Chassidic master in his own right, went with his son to visit a certain city for Shabbat. The Rebbe and his son arrived in the afternoon; following the lottery, they went to the chosen host family's house. They accompanied the host to shul and returned for the Shabbat meal. Because the family wasn't that wealthy, the main course was simply *cholent*, a slow-cooked stew of meat, beans, and potatoes. Since the Rebbe was the guest of honor, he was served first. As was customary, the host's wife paused for him to taste it before serving the rest of the family. But the Rebbe did not simply taste the cholent, he wolfed down the entire bowl of it—and then, as everyone watched, puzzled, he ate one bowl after another, until he had finally finished the entire pot.

Now, Rebbe Avigdor Halberstam was not a particularly large man, so everyone was rather surprised to watch him slurp his way rapidly through bowl after bowl of cholent, spooning the food into his mouth as fast as he could, sometimes even using the ladle right from the pot, until it was all gone. His son sat staring at him, utterly embarrassed, his eyes nearly popping out of his head. He had never seen his father eat so much food in his life. The other people around the table stared too, but nobody said a word because, after all, this was a renowned Chassidic

Rebbe—so what could they say? "There must be some spiritual reason he's eating all the cholent," they whispered to each other.

Only after the Rebbe had finished the pot of cholent did he speak. "Thank you," he said. "It was delicious." He said grace after the meal, and then left the room to retire for his Shabbat nap.

After the Shabbat ended, the Rebbe thanked his host and set off with his son to return home again. Once they had left the city, his son, bursting with suspense, turned to him and said, "I don't understand. How does a little, old, hundred-twenty-five-pound man like you have the stomach to eat all that cholent? What became of you? Why the sudden need to be so incredibly rude and devour the whole pot of cholent?"

"It's very simple, my son," the Rebbe answered. "When I tasted it, I realized that the cook had accidentally put vinegar into the cholent instead of water. The cholent was so bad that if everybody had tasted it, the hostess would have been horrified. And the host would have been even more upset! He would have told the cook, 'You've embarrassed my guest, this important Chassidic Rebbe,' and then he would have fired her. Now, I happen to know that the cook is a widow who supports her family with this job. So I had to suffer a little bit and make the small self-sacrifice of eating a putrid dish in order to protect that widow, rather than embarrass her."

 TEACHING

We often have to put ourselves in a place of physical discomfort in order to avoid embarrassing or shaming somebody. According to *Chapters of Our Fathers*, one of the greatest sins a person can commit is to embarrass someone else in public and cause that person to lose his or her share in the world to come. Besides avoiding embarrassing anyone, we must care about other people's physical needs, even if that also causes us great discomfort. In this story the Rebbe knew what would happen if he did what was natural—spat out the food and said what he really thought, "Ach, this tastes terrible!" A pot of cholent made of distilled vinegar probably tastes like ammonia! Yet the Rebbe fully understood what the ramifications would be if he didn't eat the cholent: The widowed cook would lose her livelihood and her children would suffer. Protecting other people's material comfort is so important that it is well worth our own suffering.

Is It Better to Eat a Little or a Lot?

Two of the greatest Chassidic masters—Rebbe Avraham Yehosh-ua Heshel of Apt, known as the Apter Rov, and Reb Mordechai Twersky of Chernobyl, known as the Chernobyler Maggid—had very different ways and modes of serving God. In many ways, they seemed to contradict each other: The Apter Rov served God through overeating, while Reb Mordechai ate only a few morsels of bread each day and drank only a few drops of water as his mode of service to God.

One Friday, Reb Mordechai ended up in the city of Apt, where he was invited to dine with the Apter Rov. Seated at the table together, Reb Mordechai ate a few morsels of food and sat back, finished with his dinner. The Apter Rov followed suit, eating just a few morsels of bread, and then he stopped too. Reb Mordechai turned to him and said, "I don't understand—isn't it your custom to overeat on Shabbat?"

"The holy Shabbat is a great host," responded the Apter Rov. "Whenever it's accompanied by a holiday, the holy Shabbat allows the guests to shine during prayers and the reading of the Torah. Therefore, since today's holy Shabbat is being so nice to its guests, I have to mimic it and be gracious to the guests as well."

 TEACHING

Every individual is different, so therefore our modes of service and relation-ship with the Almighty are different too. One person may pray for a long time, while another may pray for a shorter time. One may be more enthusiastic about giving charity, yet another may be less enthusiastic. But we all should recognize that when we perform a mitzvah, we aren't only doing it for ourselves, we're also doing it for the collective "we," the community.

A discourse from the Lubavitcher Rebbe tells us that when we perform a mitzvah with enthusiasm and energy, we can actually give *chayut*, or vitality, and invigorate another person who struggles with the same mitzvah through our own performance of it.

When the Jewish people stood together at Mount Sinai, we became responsible for one another. The burden of Torah is an individual as well as a communal responsibility. Therefore, whenever we perform a specific mitzvah, we must realize that we're performing that mitzvah to make it easier for other people to perform it as well.

A MESSY MENSCH

O NCE RABBI Akiva Eiger invited a poor man to join him as his guest at Shabbat, and they walked together to the rabbi's house after shul. The rabbi's home had been fully prepared for Shabbat. It was immaculate—the candles were lit and glowing, the table was set beautifully with the Kiddush cups shining, and the challah bread was still warm from the oven.

Rabbi Akiva poured a cup of wine for his guest and then poured his own, but as he did, his guest moved nervously and knocked over his own cup, spilling wine on the fresh, white tablecloth. The blood rushed to the man's face and the rabbi watched him cower with embarrassment.

Immediately, Rabbi Akiva pretended to reach for something on the table and knocked over his own Kiddush cup, too, letting the wine spill.

"This table is very shaky tonight," Rabbi Akiva calmly told the man and proceeded to set their cups upright again and refill them, thereby preventing any embarrassment for the guest at his table.

 TEACHING

In addition to the commandment of loving thy neighbor, which includes sparing the feelings of others, there is the Kabbalistic concept of *yereh boshes*, the sense of awe and fear we may experience in the presence of God. Here, a person is so humbled, it's as if they were embarrassed in public. This is not a negative trait but a high level of spirituality, difficult to reach, in which one is totally nullified in the presence of the greatness of God. When we experience yereh boshes, we have such an awe and love of God that the very thought of losing our connection to Him frightens us, and we are embarrassed by those things within us that separate us from Him. We are so shaken to the core by God that we do not ever want to be disconnected from Him, not even for a moment.

PART 2

Recipes

Cooking (and Eating) to Connect to God

A FRIEND of mine once toured the African jungle in a jeep and, like his fellow tourists, he photographed the many beautiful animals he saw. Eventually, his group came upon a pride of lions relaxing in the sun. Right away, the tourists began clapping, hooting, and shouting to get the lions to look their way for photos, but the lions just continued to laze on the ground, ignoring the raucous commotion.

"I'll show you how to get the lions' attention!" the tour guide announced, opening his travel bag and reaching inside. My friend assumed the guide would pull out a horn to blow loudly at the lions, but instead, what he took out was a pair of attached strips of Velcro, which he held out in front of him and pulled apart, making a ripping sound. Immediately, the leader of the pride, the king of that land, picked up his head and looked around as if to ask, "What was *that*?!"

Smiling broadly, the guide reattached the Velcro strips and pulled them apart a second time. This time, all the lions picked up their heads and looked around for the source of that tiny little noise—and the tourists got their photo opp.

Like my friend on the safari, we are all conditioned to believe that in order for God to notice us, we must do something big and dramatic. But in truth, small, seemingly insignificant, daily activities—like cooking, sharing, and eating food—can just as easily get the Almighty's attention.

For me, food is one of life's greatest joys, and I have fond memories of being a young child helping out in the kitchen at home and at school. But as I grew up, food also allowed me to explore my faith. I learned about Judaism through my family's Shabbat dinners. Every Friday night we gathered together for an elaborate feast that began with two freshly baked loaves of challah and my father saying the Kiddush prayer over the wine, sanctifying the end of the week and marking the transition from the mundane to the spiritual. With the Shabbat meal, we began drawing down blessings for the upcoming week.

I also learned much from celebrating the Jewish holidays with my family. Throughout the year, we celebrate our faith by eating specially prescribed dishes.

Every spring, at Passover, the oldest Jewish holiday and the grandest one of the year, we eat matzah and avoid any leavened products.

Forty-nine days later, as spring turns to summer, the holiday of Shavuot takes place. We commemorate God's giving the Torah to the Jewish people on the slopes of Mount Sinai by receiving it anew, and we celebrate by partaking of dairy foods like blintzes and cheesecake.

In September we celebrate Rosh Hashanah, the Jewish New Year. As we begin the ten days of penitence that culminate in Yom Kippur, the Day of Atonement, we enjoy many delicacies, including sweet foods to mark a sweet new year; part of the head of a fish; seasonal fruits like pomegranates; and various types of vegetables, each of which has special meaning and signifies specific intentions for the year to come. Finally, on the eve of the holiday of Yom Kippur we fulfill the mitzvah of eating well, and then on the holiday itself we fast.

Four days after Yom Kippur, we move from the most serious and introspective time of the year to one of the most joyous and cheerful. The holiday of Sukkot, which lasts a week, commemorates the annual agricultural harvest and the forty years in which the Jewish people wandered through the desert, living in temporary shelters. For Sukkot, we gather with our friends and family to eat rich, beautifully prepared dishes in a designated place: our sukkah, a hut that we build each year ourselves. On the last day of the holiday, Simchat Torah, we eat *kreplach*, Jewish dumplings, to commemorate the end of the annual cycle of public Torah readings and the beginning of a new cycle. We also drink many l'chaims, or toasts.

In December, for the eight nights of Chanukah, the festival of lights, we enjoy a variety of cheeses as well as many rich, oily, fried foods like *latkes* and jelly donuts, or *sufganiyot*.

In the dead of winter, on Tu BiShvat, also known as "the new year for trees," we mark the emergence of the earliest blooming trees from their winter sleep in the land of Israel by enjoying the *sheva minim*, the seven foods that were the only acceptable offerings in the Temple: wheat, barley, grapes, figs, pomegranates, olives (and olive oil), and dates (or honey).

Finally, on Purim, celebrated at the end of winter, we commemorate the saving of the Jewish people from the wicked King Haman, who planned to destroy all the Jews in a single day, by baking and eating sweet Hamantaschen cookies filled with dates, poppy seeds, halvah, or jam. To spread the joy of the holiday, we also give away ready-to-eat food to at least one of our friends, symbolizing the miracle that took place concealed within nature.

But there are even more connections between Judaism and food than those evident in holiday traditions. As a child learning the Torah, I noticed that food frequently appears in its stories. Adam and Eve's sin is connected to eating. Abraham makes a treaty with the king of the Philistines involving seven female lambs to be eaten in return for Abraham's friendship. The Jewish people, enduring a forty-year exile in the desert without a home, are graced with manna raining down from Heaven. In Genesis, after the flood God tells Noah that every moving thing upon the earth—fish, fowl, animals, green plants—will be mankind's food; later, Noah plants a vineyard and becomes drunk and merry from the wine he makes from the grapes he harvests.

Of all the world's ethnicities, societies, and religions, Judaism has the most numerous and specific laws regarding how and when food is to be prepared and eaten. The relationship between food and the Torah fills me with wonder. The book of Leviticus lays out Judaism's dietary laws, or kashrut, including what makes certain foods kosher, but other foods not. For instance, a fish is kosher when it has fins and a certain style of scales; meat is kosher only from animals with split hooves that chew their cud; certain birds are kosher, but an enumerated list of them is not permitted; and it is forbidden to eat insects, rodents, and blood. Kashrut also discusses the prohibition against cooking and eating meat and dairy together, and explains in great detail the proper slaughtering process and the preparation of meat.

When I began studying Kabbalah, I learned that everything created in this world contains a spark of God within it, giving it its life force. Therefore, every time we eat of the food God gives us, if we do so with the proper preparations and in the proper context, we have the power to elevate the spark of God within that food; through the physical act of eating, we can raise food up to God.

Food is such a front-row event in the daily practices of a religious Jew that knowing about the Kabbalistic connection between God and food leads to a deeper understanding. Not only can we elevate the spark of God within food, but we can also embrace the physical and use it to make a dwelling place for God. As the Ba'al Shem Tov explains, the physical is a fundamental aspect of how we can cause excitement and commotion in the heavenly realms.

God promised Abraham that when his children found themselves strangers in a land that wasn't theirs, He would redeem them. After the Jewish people were slaves in Egypt for 210 years, God decided it was time to save them; nevertheless, they still needed to deserve to be freed. There is a *midrash* that says that although while living in Egypt the Jewish people assimilated in many ways—despite abandoning some Jewish customs, they proudly maintained three aspects of their identity: their Hebrew names, their Hebrew language, and their mode of dress. But there's another opinion that says that the third vital thing the Jewish people maintained in Egypt was their kosher food style—not their clothing.

As Jews, our quest is to embrace the physical world, mainly through food, to come to know God. That's what brought me to writing this book. Nothing makes me happier than cooking for my family and friends, gathering around the table, and sharing a meal. But as much as I love food, I also love Chassidic tales. The sixth Lubavitcher Rebbe, Rabbi Yosef Yitzchak Schneerson, notes in the *Hayam Yom*, that hearing a story allows the listener "to experience a penetrating realization ... of one's deepest inwardness."

The Chassidic tales hold great power because "every narrative is a lesson in life," the Rebbe writes. "Every story must bring forth for the listener a fine character trait" such as the righteousness of the tzaddikim, and "an inner enthusiasm for the beauty of the mitzvah..." Each story, he writes, "should engender a profound appreciation of the ways of pleasantness of Chassidic teachings."

Since food is at the very heart of Judaism, it's not surprising that many Chassidic tales are centered around cooking and eating. This book combines some of my favorite Chassidic stories about food with recipes from my own kitchen for dishes that my family enjoys at our Shabbat table and on holidays. I hope these stories whet my readers' appetites and help them begin elevating the spark of godliness in what they eat in order to make the physical world a dwelling place for the Almighty.

—*Rabbi Hanoch Hecht*

The Jewish Holidays at a Glance

From the perspective of Jewish law, observances, and customs, the holidays are very different from Shabbat. Although many of the practices are similar—we go to synagogue and listen to a Torah reading, and then come back home and have a festive meal—holidays nevertheless represent a different level of spiritual energy and holiness, so the customs vary. For instance, on the holy Shabbat day it is forbidden to cook, so we eat precooked dishes, such as cholent, to adhere to those laws.

But when it comes to the holidays, although we are not permitted to make fire, we are permitted to cook food because we are allowed to partake of the things from which the body receives benefit. Jewish holidays are times for joy (simcha) and even though Shabbat is a time of enjoyment and pleasure, it still doesn't carry with it the level of simcha that a holiday does. The verse is written, "And you should rejoice in your holiday." We go out of our way to make dishes for the holidays that are even more special than the ones we make for a regular Shabbat to enhance our enjoyment of the holiday.

- **Passover or Pesach:** God's liberation of the Israelites from Egyptian bondage is the most theologically important holiday in the Jewish calendar. Passover takes place in late March or April and lasts for eight days.
- **Shavuot:** Coming forty-nine days after Passover, Shavuot celebrates the giving of the Torah at Mount Sinai. In the time of the First Temple in Jerusalem, farmers brought the first fruits of their four-year-old trees.
- **Rosh Hashanah:** This solemn holiday, celebrated in mid-to-late September, marks the beginning of the Jewish year and the crowning of God as King of the Universe.
- **Yom Kippur:** The Day of Atonement is one of fasting and confession following a celebratory dinner on the eve of Yom Kippur, observed in the early-to-mid autumn.
- **Sukkot:** We celebrate Sukkot by going into handmade huts for a week and performing the special Mitzvah of the Four Species by gathering and waving four plants specified in the Torah. When the Temple stood in Jerusalem, the Jewish people made a week-long pilgrimage there to celebrate the harvest. The holiday still coincides with the harvest, taking place in mid-autumn.
- **Simchat Torah:** At the close of Sukkot, there is one more holiday, which celebrates completing the annual reading of the Torah scroll for the year and starting it over again.
- **Chanukah:** This eight-day holiday commemorates the Jewish recapture and rededication of the Temple in Jerusalem in 164 BCE, when the oil in the Temple's lamps miraculously burned for eight days. Chanukah is celebrated in December.
- **Tu B'Shevat:** "The Birthday of Trees" is the day on which we celebrate the buds of the fruits appearing on the trees in the land of Israel.
- **Purim:** The celebration of the Jewish people's narrow escape from genocide at the hands of the evil Haman, as described in the book of Esther. Purim usually takes place in March, coinciding with winter's close and spring's beginning.

Shabbat Recipes

God created the world in six days. After He created the entire physical world, He asked, "What is the world lacking?" God determined that the world was lacking rest, so He created the holy Shabbat day. Now, *rest* doesn't mean putting your feet up on a couch and watching television all day. It means taking time out from the mundane and having a day of spirituality and godliness, of returning to God. When it comes to Shabbat, we celebrate on the physical plane by wearing nice clothing and indulging in the pleasures of eating and drinking. On the spiritual plane, we celebrate by studying, praying, and removing ourselves from many of the activities we normally undertake during the week.

- Challah
- Yummy Pesto Butter
- Dill-Encrusted Salmon
- Moroccan Salmon
- Sephardic Spicy Fish
- Classic Gefilte Fish Balls
- Spicy Gefilte Fish Balls
- Baked Chicken
- Chicken Liver with Mushroom Sauce
- Sephardic Chicken
- Chicken Schnitzel
- Chicken Soup
- Matzah Balls for Chicken Soup
- Fried Broccoli
- Cholent
- Kishke
- Potato Kugel

Challah

This special bread is baked every Friday in Jewish homes, to be eaten on the holy Shabbat day, which begins at sundown on Friday and continues until nightfall on Saturday. The word "challah" actually means "portion," based on the commandment that whenever bread is baked, the baker must take off a portion and give it away to the priest as charity. Today, we separate a portion of the challah and burn it.

Yields 4 medium loaves of challah

Ingredients

1 ⅓ cup warm water

1 teaspoon honey

1 tablespoon dry yeast

4½ cups kosher flour (bread flour is preferred, but all-purpose flour or a mixture of half bread flour and half whole wheat flour can be used)

2 eggs

⅓ cup oil

½ cup honey

2 generous pinches of salt

Optional: Poppy seeds, sesame seeds, or zaatar

Procedure

Proof the yeast with water and honey for 2 minutes, then knead the ingredients together and allow to rise for 1 hour or until twice the size.

Divide into four equal portions.

Shape the loaves into rounds or braids and give them an additional 30 minutes to rise.

Brush with room-temperature egg wash. If the egg wash is too cold, it could cause the dough to fall. If desired, sprinkle with seeds or zaatar.

Bake at 350° for 25 to 30 minutes—checking after 20 minutes—or until golden brown.

Yummy Pesto Butter

At our home, we love hot challah, so before Shabbat, we wrap most of our challah with foil and place it in the oven to warm it thoroughly for the meal. A spread of pesto butter complements the warm challah beautifully. It's divine!

Although pesto is traditionally made with pine nuts, I use slivered almonds because they are less expensive and more readily available.

Ingredients

1 cup basil (about 20 leaves)
¼ cup olive oil
⅓ cup slivered almonds
3 cloves garlic

½ stick margarine or butter
1 teaspoon pepper
1 tablespoon salt

Procedure

In a food processor, add all of the ingredients except the oil, blending each one slowly until the mixture reaches a pasty, spreadable consistency. Add the oil last, pouring it in very slowly.

If you are using pesto for a meal at which meat will be served, substitute margarine for butter as per kosher law so as not to mix meat and milk together.

Fish

Eating kosher fish helps us erect a spiritual shield around ourselves. In ancient times, when soldiers went to war they wore shields made out of little metal scales to protect them from harm; so too, when we venture out into the physical world we need to create a shield of spiritual scales protecting us from any harm.

Fins allow fish to swim against the water current. Sometimes the performance of mitzvot or keeping to Jewish law is not easy, and one has to swim against the tide and have the pride and strength to do what's right.

Jewish recipes for fish dishes range widely in style. In 1948, when the State of Israel was formed, Ashkenazic and Eastern European Jews left war-torn Europe to emigrate there; over the decades since, Jews from many different countries in the Middle East and North Africa emigrated there as well to escape the anti-Semitism developing in their countries.

As a result, Israel is a veritable cholent pot, mixing bowl, of Jewish people from very different lands and walks of life, with a wide variety of customs and halachic authorities influencing them. Some of the communities from which Jews have emigrated to Israel date back 2,000 years or more, and while many of the Ashkenazic Jews from Eastern Europe had adopted the modern European style of dress, the Sephardic Jews usually arrived wearing traditional garb.

Over time, however, the Sephardic Jews began to give up their customs to modernize and follow Ashkenazic ways of living; the Lubavitcher Rebbe began emphasizing the importance of each group of Jews keeping true to its heritage and maintaining its customs. As we well know, when the Jews left Egypt, there were twelve tribes, each with a unique relationship to God that affected their daily service and prayers. The Lubavitcher Rebbe recognized that it was crucial to maintain these customs in order to keep the twelve tribes alive. In Jewish cuisine, fish offers one of the best examples of how the many regions in which Jews have lived during the diaspora have influenced the preparation of a single given food.

DILL-ENCRUSTED SALMON

A note to the home cook: Some people buy salmon in pre-sliced portions. Although these fillets may be very tasty, cooking a *whole side* of salmon retains more of its fattiness and is more flavorful. When choosing salmon, look for white, fatty lines in between the flesh. The thicker the lines are, the more flavor the salmon will have.

Serves 12; for a smaller crowd, use half a side of salmon

INGREDIENTS

½ bunch fresh dill, chopped finely

3 cloves garlic, crushed

Salt, according to your liking

Pepper, according to your liking

3 tablespoons olive oil

Wax or parchment paper

PROCEDURE

Lay the entire side of salmon on a tray and pat it dry.

Sprinkle it with salt and pepper.

Combine the chopped dill, garlic, and olive oil in a bowl and mix well, then spread evenly over the entire salmon.

Place wax paper or parchment paper over the salmon and let it sit for 30 minutes in the refrigerator.

Remove the wax paper and bake at 400° for 30 minutes.

Serve hot or cold.

Moroccan Salmon

Since the destruction of the first temple in Jerusalem by the Babylonians, about 2,500 years ago, the Jewish people have been living in a diaspora. Many were dispersed throughout the Middle East and Morocco, housing the largest Jewish population in the Muslim world. At its peak, the Moroccan Jewish community numbered between 250,000 and 350,000.

However, since 1948, when the State of Israel was created, many Jews have left Morocco for Israel, and by 2017 the Moroccan Jewish community numbered less than 3,000. The Jews who live in Morocco today practice their religion in a free and open way because the current Moroccan king, Mohammed VI, is friendly toward them; however, Moroccan Jews also maintain a quiet presence because many of their neighbors do not support the State of Israel.

This salmon recipe is typically served in Moroccan Jewish homes for Shabbat dinner. Of course, each *safta* (bubbe) has her own way of making it; this is my safta's recipe.

Serves 6 to 8

Ingredients

Marinade
½ cup oil
2 tablespoons paprika
¼ bunch parsley, chopped
1 tablespoon salt
1 teaspoon pepper, freshly ground
1 teaspoon garlic powder
½ teaspoon crushed red pepper
1 tomato, grated
5 fillets of salmon

Sauté
1 tablespoon frying oil

1 onion
3 red peppers, chopped
½ jalapeño pepper, sliced into thin circles
3 cloves of garlic, sliced
1 teaspoon salt
1 tablespoon paprika

Finishing
1 tablespoon lemon juice
¼ bunch parsley, chopped
1 small can (about 6 oz.) or ½ large can (about 12 oz.) of chickpeas, drained

Marinate the salmon fillets in a bowl with the oil, paprika, parsley, salt, pepper, garlic powder, crushed red pepper, and grated tomatoes for 30 minutes.

Heat the oil over medium heat and sauté the onion until translucent. Add the peppers; after three minutes of sautéing, add the garlic, salt, and paprika and cook until the peppers are tender.

Add the marinated salmon to the pan and cook for 10 minutes.

Add the lemon juice, the rest of the parsley, and the chickpeas.

Simmer, covered, on low heat for 20 minutes. Serve hot.

Sephardic Spicy Fish

According to Kabbalah, the Hebrew alphabet is not just a means of communication: Each of the twenty-two letters has a numerical value that corresponds to its shape, sound, and spiritual energy—and so too, each word contains a value that is the sum of its letters.

The names of the foods served on the holy Sabbath day correspond with the number seven, because the Sabbath occurs on the seventh day of the week. So it is no accident that we eat fish for Shabbat. The Hebrew word for fish is *dag*, which contains the Hebrew letters *dalet*, which has a numerical value of four, and *gimmel*, which has a numerical value of three; together, they add up to seven.

Serves 6

Ingredients

5 pieces of 4-oz. fillets of salmon or Chilean sea bass

1 onion

3 cloves of fresh garlic

1 red pepper

1 yellow pepper

3 vine tomatoes

1 tablespoon salt

1 jalapeño pepper

Olive oil

Spice mix

1 teaspoon each of paprika, turmeric, salt, black pepper, and chili pepper, mixed together

1 pinch of saffron

Procedure

Slice the onion and fry with olive oil in a skillet until translucent.

Slice the garlic, peppers, and tomatoes and add them to the skillet.

Cover and let simmer for 10 minutes.

Add the spice mix and let simmer for an additional 10 minutes.

Add the fish and saffron and cook for 30 minutes, basting every 5 minutes.

Serve hot.

Gefilte Fish, Served Two Ways

On the Holy Shabbat Day, it's important to experience proper *oneg*, pleasure, with the meal. That is why we eat fish followed by meat. In many of the poor Ashkenazi communities of old, gefilte fish was traditionally eaten on Shabbat, stuffed into the skin of a larger fish, as the word *gefilte* means "stuffed."

I like to offer my guests both Classic Gefilte Fish Balls and contemporary Spicy Gefilte Fish Balls.

Classic Gefilte Fish Balls

Yields 10 to 12 fish balls (or can be served as a loaf)

Ingredients

1 small onion	1 tablespoon pepper
1 whole carrot	1 package of gefilte fish roll, defrosted
½ cup sugar	Optional: Any additional spices
1 teaspoon salt	that delight the palate

Procedure

Mix the onion, carrot, sugar, salt, and pepper into 8 cups of water and bring to a boil.

To make the fish balls, wet your hands and shape a small amount of defrosted fish into a ball.

When the water comes to a boil, add the 10 gefilte fish balls and cook, covered, for 30 minutes.

You may also add fish bones to make the broth more gelatinous, and any additional spices, to the water initially to give the stock more flavor.

Spicy Gefilte Fish Balls

Yields 10 to 12 fish balls

Ingredients

28 oz. canned tomato puree

28 oz. canned diced tomatoes

1 onion, diced

3 cloves garlic, minced

1 chili or habanero pepper

1 yellow pepper

1 tablespoon salt

1 teaspoon dried basil

1 teaspoon dried parsley

1 bay leaf

1 teaspoon garlic powder

¼ teaspoon pepper

Procedure

Make 10 to 12 Classic Gefilte Fish balls and set aside.

In a large pan, sauté the diced onions, covered, over medium heat, until translucent.

Add the garlic and sauté for 1 minute.

Add the diced peppers and sauté for 6 minutes.

Add the diced tomatoes, tomato puree, and spices and bring to a steady simmer.

Add the fish balls to the pot and cook for 30 to 45 minutes over low heat.

Stir occasionally so the balls don't stick to the pot.

Serve hot or cold.

MEAT AND DAIRY

When it comes to kashrut, the body of Jewish religious laws concerning the suitability of food, the strictest prohibition in Torah, is against the mixing together of milk and meat or fowl. God gave us a special commandment regarding this. This observance is so severe that following the laws properly requires using two sets of dishes and utensils to prevent any possibility of mixing milk and meat or fowl together.

Through Kabbalah and Chassidut, we can comprehend some of the mystical aspects of this prohibition. Meat (or fowl) represents a certain kind of spiritual energy. It is the flesh of an animal whose life has been given up for us. Dairy represents an opposite form of spiritual energy, having to do with birth and the nurturance of young life. Combining dairy with meat creates a kind of spiritual explosion to which the soul is highly allergic. Just as in the physical world, if someone takes two chemicals and combines them, a certain reaction occurs, when we digest certain foods, our bodies as well as our souls react.

As the old saying goes, "You are what you eat." In other words, the food we eat turns into our very flesh and blood. So why is it that the Torah names split hooves and chewed cud as criteria for a kosher animal? Or, better yet, what positive qualities do animals that have split hooves and chew their cud represent that we therefore must emulate?

One of the reasons given in Kabbalah for eating animals with split hooves, like the cow, is that when dealing with the physical we must have a dual approach: On one hand, we must be above the ground and in some level removed from the physical world, but on the other hand, we are given the mission to elevate the physical world by dealing with it.

Chewed cud represents the concept that no matter how well we feel we have elevated the physical, we must elevate it again. Just as a cow chews its food over and over again to digest it, so we must constantly refine and purify the physical world many times over, each day, on a new and higher level.

Chicken is a standard dish on the Shabbat table. Here are my favorite chicken recipes for Shabbat: Baked Chicken, Chicken Liver with Mushroom Sauce, Sephardic Chicken, Chicken Schnitzel, and Chicken Soup with Matzah Balls.

Baked Chicken

In the Book of Isaiah, the Jewish people are enjoined to "call the Sabbath a delight." Shabbat is therefore designated for enjoyment, and the Shabbat dinner must include a fish course followed by a course that features some kind of meat or chicken. In my family, baked chicken is a popular second course.

Serves 8

Ingredients

1 large sweet potato

1 chicken, cut into 8 pieces

1 cup of water

Spice Rub

1 teaspoon salt

1 teaspoon black pepper

1 teaspoon garlic powder

1 teaspoon onion powder

1 teaspoon dried parsley

1 teaspoon sweet paprika

Optional: 1 teaspoon cayenne pepper

Procedure

Preheat the oven for 375°.

Mix together the spices and set aside. If you prefer spicy chicken, feel free to add 1 teaspoon cayenne pepper to the spice rub.

Peel the sweet potato and slice it, then use it to line a baking tray.

Pour 1 cup of water into the tray.

Place the chicken on top of the sweet potato slices and sprinkle the spice rub on top.

Bake for 50 minutes.

CHICKEN LIVER WITH MUSHROOM SAUCE

There is a biblical prohibition against eating blood. Since all meat from animals is flesh containing blood within it, the kosher process of washing and soaking the meat for 30 minutes both ensures that the blood is removed from the exterior and softens the flesh. Then, covering the meat with rough-grain salt and letting it sit for an hour draws the rest of the blood out of the meat. With liver, the kosher process is even more important because the function of the liver is to cleanse the blood. Therefore, grilling salted liver on an open fire with Xs cut into its flesh is the only way to make sure that the liver is kosher.

Serves 8

INGREDIENTS

1 lb. chicken liver

1 medium onion, sliced into circles

10 mushrooms (preferably cremini), sliced

Pinch of salt

1 teaspoon black pepper

1 teaspoon red wine vinegar

PROCEDURE

After the liver has been prepared in kosher fashion, sauté the onion in a saucepan until translucent.

Add the sliced mushrooms and cook over medium-high heat.

Add the seasoning and stir until the mushrooms and onions are caramelized.

Pour in the red wine vinegar.

When the mixture is golden brown, pour it over the chicken liver and toss. Serve cold.

Sephardic Chicken

Sephardic Jews have incorporated into their recipes the many different spices and dried fruits that are unique to the regions of North Africa and the Middle East. This Sephardic chicken recipe includes dates, which are a staple of the Sephardic Jewish kitchen.

Serves 4 to 8

Ingredients

1 chicken, cut into 8 pieces

10 medjool dates, pitted and sliced

2 tablespoons honey

1 tablespoon black pepper

Procedure

Preheat oven to 325°.

Lay the chicken out in a deep roasting pan. Drizzle honey over it. Sprinkle with black pepper and dates.

Bake covered for 2 hours.

Chicken Schnitzel

We tend to think of Israeli food as having Middle Eastern origins, but schnitzel, which is a popular Israeli street food, was actually brought to Israel by European Jews. In fact, schnitzel got its name from the Old German word *snidan*, which means "to cut," since schnitzel is made with cutlets. On the streets of Israel today, each falafel and shawarma stand offers schnitzel as well. Schnitzel is a great example of how the Jews in Israel may be from different countries but they all come together through eating—enjoying foods from around the world served in a pita.

Serves 8

INGREDIENTS

4 chicken cutlets
½ cup flour
½ cup panko breadcrumbs
1 cup matzah meal
½ cup cornflakes, ground fine
2 eggs
1 tablespoon water
Oil for frying

Seasoning

1 teaspoon salt
1 teaspoon dried parsley
1 teaspoon black pepper

PROCEDURE

Slice the chicken cutlets in half to ¼-inch thickness and tenderize them with a mallet.

Place the cutlets in a 1-gallon ziplock plastic bag. Add the flour and shake well until the cutlets are covered thoroughly.

Set aside two bowls.

In one bowl, beat together the eggs and water.

In the other bowl, make a dry topping by mixing well together the panko breadcrumbs, ground cornflakes, and seasonings.

Remove the floured chicken from the plastic bag and submerge each cutlet into the egg batter, then into the dry topping, making sure it's covered well.

Lay the cutlets out flat on a tray.

Cover the bottom of a saucepan with oil. Fry each side of the schnitzel on medium-high heat until golden brown.

Chicken Soup

I've never met anyone who hasn't said that their mother's chicken soup is the best-tasting one they've ever had. So, of course, here is my own mother's recipe!

Serves 10

Ingredients

Water to fill a 5-quart pot (or larger)

2 carrots, peeled and chopped

1 stalk of celery, chopped

1 small unpeeled sweet potato, chopped

½ leek, washed well

¼ bunch of dill

1 onion, with skin left on

2 pieces of chicken or 1 piece of chicken and 6 chicken necks

2 tablespoons salt

Pinch of black pepper

Procedure

Slice off the top and bottom of the onion, but leave the skin on.

Add the onion and all of the other ingredients to the pot of water and bring it to a boil. After 30 minutes skim the top of the soup. Cook covered for 3½ hours at a rolling boil.

Matzah Balls for Chicken Soup

Matzahs are famously associated with Passover, but in many homes, Chicken Soup with Matzah Balls is also a standard Shabbat dish.

For Chassidics, the preparation of matzahs also involves a very important ceremony. We don't eat regular, commercially-produced kosher matzahs, we eat *shmurah* matzahs, which are round, kneaded, hand-shaped matzahs harvested with great care taken to avoid any moisture. Shmurah means to be guarded, and never to come in contact with water. So, from the planting of the wheat in fields that are always guarded, through its harvesting, and right up until the matzahs are baked—we are very, very careful that the wheat, and later the flour, has no contact with water.

In Lubavitch, there was a farmer by the name of Zalman of Chervin, who was a great scholar and had tremendous knowledge of the Chassidic teachings and philosophy. However, when it came to performing the mitzvah of producing matzahs, his knowledge surpassed anyone else's. He understood that grain needs to be harvested at a specific point. If it's harvested too early or too late, that can hasten the process of the grains becoming leavened, so the harvesting must be done at the perfect time in late summer. For every harvest, Zalman of Chervin would go a few weeks beforehand into the shtetl, round up volunteers, load them into wagons, and take them back to his farm. It was a great honor to be chosen to participate and a very happy time for the volunteers. In the wagons on the way back to the farm they would celebrate by singing *niginim*, Chassidic melodies.

Then, when the day of harvesting arrived, Reb Zalman, even in his later years, would go out with his wife and his children and harvest the grain themselves, taking a sickle to cut the stalks—and the Chassidim who were volunteering to help would sing and dance as they collected the grains. The whole process was a great celebration, and when they had finished collecting the grain, Reb Zalman prepared a huge feast and served it out in the fields and the orchards, and everybody ate and danced to music.

After the flour, the second-most important ingredient in matzahs is water. But not just any water can be used. The Chassidim call this special water *mayim shelanu*, which means "our water." The night before they baked the matzahs, they would go out to the well and draw the water that would be used. But once again, this was not done quietly, but rather with great fanfare. The Chassidim would put on their *kaputas*, long coats; their *shtreimels*, fur hats; and their *gartels*, sashes, and they would dance and sing as they hauled the water.

Traditionally, even the hard parts of making the matzah involved great festivity. In fact, the story is told of an elderly Chassidic rebbe who, one harvest season, was on his way down to the river to collect the water for mayim shelanu and was being followed by his Chassidim, who were singing and dancing. Along came a wagon carrying one of his colleagues. "Why don't you hop on the wagon?" his friend asked. But even though the Chassidic master was in his eighties, he turned around and answered his friend, "No, thank you! You think I would allow the horses and the wagon to take away my reward for trudging down through the mud to get the water?"

Yields 8 matzah balls

Ingredients

¾ cup matzah meal

3 tablespoons seltzer

2 eggs

1 tablespoon oil

2 tablespoons baking soda

Chicken soup mix

2 tablespoons salt

4 quarts water

Procedure

Boil a pot of water seasoned with chicken soup mix or salt.

Mix the batter together (matzah meal, seltzer, eggs, oil, and baking soda), and allow it to sit in the refrigerator for an hour.

Oil your hands and form the batter into golf ball-sized balls. Allow the matzah balls to cook in a rolling boil for 30 minutes.

Remove from water and place the completely cooked matzah balls into the chicken soup before serving.

Note: Never cook matzah balls in the actual chicken soup because they fall apart and turn the broth cloudy.

FRIED BROCCOLI

My sister-in-law is from a Sephardic family originally based in Libya, and her family has made this dish for generations. It is one of my favorite dishes to enjoy whenever I am lucky enough to be at her home for a Shabbat. I have created my own dipping sauce for this dish, which I serve on the side.

Serves 8

INGREDIENTS

1½ pounds fresh broccoli, chopped and boiled until tender, or 16-oz. package frozen chopped broccoli, defrosted

½ cup flour

1 cup water

1 tablespoon salt

1 teaspoon pepper

½ teaspoon cayenne pepper

¼ cup oil for frying

Dipping Sauce

2 tablespoons rice wine vinegar

1 tablespoon soy sauce

1 tablespoon honey

1 teaspoon sesame oil

1 tablespoon fresh chives, chopped

PROCEDURE

Mix the dipping sauce ingredients, stirring well, and set aside.

Chop the broccoli into bite-sized pieces and set aside in a bowl.

Mix the flour and water to create a paste. Add the flour paste and the spices to the chopped broccoli and mix well.

Oil a large frying pan. Ladle broccoli into the pan as you would pancake batter. Fry the broccoli patties until each one is golden brown on both sides.

Serve warm with dipping sauce on the side.

Cholent

In observance of the Sabbath, there are thirty-nine general prohibitions that are forbidden on Shabbat. All of them are derived from the construction of the Tabernacle when the Jewish people lived in the desert. Eleven of these prohibitions are connected to the making of bread, from working the ground in which the wheat is grown, to preparing and baking the dough.

All of the prohibitions were set down in relation to Creation. Since God created the world in six days and then rested on the seventh, so must we work for six days and then take a day off from our labors, similar to God resting after creation. Therefore, on the Sabbath we are prohibited from cooking. But it has also been customary for the past 2,000 years to eat hot food on the Sabbath. Cholent is a meal that allows us to avoid cooking on the Sabbath but still have hot food. Cholent is a slow-cooked stew which differs in ingredients and style from one region or community to another.

Serves 8

Ingredients

2 cups mixed dried beans: a combination of red kidney beans, black-eyed peas, and navy beans
½ cup pearl barley
¼ large sweet potato
2 tablespoons hot paprika
1 tablespoon sweet paprika

1 teaspoon turmeric
1 teaspoon black pepper
1 tablespoon kosher salt
2 tablespoon ketchup or BBQ sauce
1 tablespoon honey
1 large red potato
Water to fill pot

Procedure

Soak the beans in cold water overnight.

Add all of the ingredients to a 5-quart slow cooker or crockpot. Cook on high for 3 hours, then turn to low to cook overnight. Cholent should cook for a minimum of 12 hours.

(Note: A regular pot on the stove can also be used, but be careful not to let the cholent burn.)

KISHKE

The word *kishke* means intestines. Traditionally, this dish's ingredients were stuffed into intestines and cooked, but kishke is no longer stuffed into intestines. Today it's common to add kishke to cholent, but kishke can also be eaten plain and meatless (*pareve*), or with gravy poured over it, and served hot.

Yields 8 slices

INGREDIENTS

1 onion
1 carrot
1 stalk celery
½ sweet potato, peeled
1 tablespoon salt
1 teaspoon pepper
1 teaspoon paprika

1 teaspoon hot paprika or chili powder
1 teaspoon garlic powder
1 teaspoon onion powder
⅓ cup oil
1½ cups all-purpose flour
Parchment paper

PROCEDURE

Using a food processor with the fine grater attachment, grate the onion, carrot, celery, and sweet potato. Add oil and regrind ingredients with a food processor, using a regular blade.

Add the spices and flour and mix in a bowl until combined.

Form the mixture into a log and wrap in parchment paper and bake at 375° for 45 minutes.

Potato Kugel

My bubbe, Soochie, was a holy woman who spent her free time saying psalms. Her six sons all became great rabbis, founding the Hecht rabbinical dynasty, which now numbers in the hundreds around the globe. Bubbe Soochie and her husband, Shea, were not from rabbinic families and did not intend for their sons to become rabbis; however, they taught their sons to be observant, even though that was not popular in the 1920s and '30s in America. This is her secret potato kugel recipe.

Yields 12 sliced squares

Ingredients

8 golden potatoes	2 tablespoons salt (or more to taste)
3 medium onions	1 tablespoon pepper
4 large eggs	¾ cup oil

Procedure

Lightly grease a 9 x 13-inch cake pan, either glass or metal.

Preheat oven to 425°. Line a 9 x 13-inch pan with parchment paper. (To make sure it sticks, wipe the pan with a drop of oil first.)

Peel and wash the potatoes. Grate the potatoes and onions using a food processor. Remove half the potato mixture and blend it again with the blade attachment.

Do not leave grated potatoes sitting or they will turn black. Have the mixture ready for adding the potatoes to it immediately after grating them, then mix well and spread evenly in the pan.

In a bowl, combine both potato mixture, oil, eggs, salt, and pepper. Mix until incorporated.

Spread mixture evenly in the pan and bake for about 90 minutes, or until the top layer is crispy brown. After 30 minutes of baking, spread 1 tablespoon of oil on top of the kugel to get a crispy-brown finish.

Passover Recipes

Passover is different from any other holiday. Its preparation literally takes weeks and begins the minute the holiday of Purim has ended. We clean our homes from top to bottom and discard any leavened products, and we stock up on the proper matzah, wine, and other ingredients. As Passover draws closer, the madness of the preparation gets more intense, but as soon as the first Seder begins, everything changes from chaos to relaxation. This is a metaphor for what our ancestors went through, moving from slavery to freedom in just one second.

- The Seder Plate
- Charoset
- Brisket
- Almond Sugar Cookies

The Seder Plate

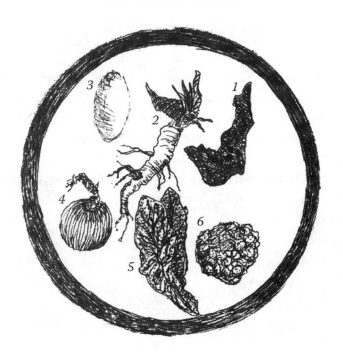

We celebrate Passover with six items on the Seder plate; moving counterclockwise from the upper right-hand section, they are as follows:

1. The *zeroah*, or shank bone, symbolizes the Pascal lamb that each family sent a member to sacrifice at the Temple in Jerusalem each year to give thanks for being freed from slavery in Egypt. After the sacrifice, each family's representative would bring their lamb back home for a barbecue. We do not eat this bone; it is there for symbolic purposes only.

2. The *maror*, or bitter herb, is usually horseradish greens or another herb that will bring cause our eyes to tear up in recollection of the bitterness of slavery.

3. Although there is no Temple today, and therefore no holiday sacrifice, the roasted egg, known as the *baytsah*, is symbolic of the fact that we are all still mourning the Temple's destruction. The egg represents the circle of life; whenever a Jewish mourner returns home from burying a loved one, the first thing he does is eat an egg.

4. The vegetable included on the plate is known as the *karpas*. Any vegetable is acceptable and is usually chosen according to geographic customs and what happens to be available. Parsley or celery are common, but many people of European ancestry use an onion simply because onions were more readily available. Whichever vegetable we use, we dip it in the saltwater provided for all in a bowl on the Seder table, to remind us of the tears our people shed in slavery.

5. The *chazeret*, or second bitter herb, is usually a piece of romaine lettuce. We eat bitter herbs twice because if we want to appreciate and celebrate our freedom, then first we need to understand slavery.

6. The final and perhaps most significant item on the Seder plate is the *charoset*. This chopped fruit-and-nut mixture represents the making of bricks and mortar, which was the most important job of the Jewish people as slaves in Egypt. Kabbalah asks, "What's so significant about mortar and bricks?" Mankind's whole purpose in this world is to build a life. There are two types of "bricks" one can use: the brick of spirituality and holiness, and the brick of impurity and unholiness. Each of us toils and inevitably builds our life in this world, but we need to use our lives to create a dwelling place for God, using the bricks of holiness.

Charoset

Charoset sits on the Seder plate to remind us of the bricks and mortar the Jewish slaves were forced to make in Egypt. Everyone uses their grandmother's charoset recipe, and this is the recipe that was handed down to me.

Serves 8

Ingredients

1 apple, peeled and grated

1 pear, peeled and grated

1 tablespoon ground walnuts

2 tablespoons ground almonds

1 cup Concord grape juice

Procedure

Add the ingredients together and allow them to sit in the refrigerator for 2 hours before serving.

BRISKET

The most popular dish served in Jewish homes for Passover, Rosh Hashanah, Yom Kippur, and other holidays is brisket. Eating brisket carries much cultural symbolism for American Jews, whose predecessors struggled to feed their families in war-torn Europe and saw America as the land of opportunity. In America, food is abundant and affordable, so for the holidays, emigrants could eat like the rich. So, for descendants of Jewish emigrants, brisket represents the lavish American lifestyle.

Serve ½ lb. per person

INGREDIENTS

1 tablespoon salt

1 teaspoon black pepper

1 teaspoon paprika

1 teaspoon garlic powder

1 teaspoon onion powder

1 large onion, sliced into circles

3 stalks of celery, sliced into ¼-inch pieces

2 carrots, peeled and sliced into ¼-inch "coins"

1 parsnip, peeled and sliced into ¼-inch coins

1 cup fresh grapefruit juice

2 cups Manischewitz or other sweet kosher wine

Brisket, weighing 12 to 18 lbs.

PROCEDURE

Sauté onions until transparent.

Add vegetables and herbs and spices and sauté 10 minutes.

Add grapefruit juice and wine and bring to a simmer.

Place brisket into roasting pan and pour the mixture over it.

Cover and cook at 300° for 10 minutes per pound, turning over the brisket every hour. Total cooking time should be 2 to 3 hours depending on the size of the brisket.

Almond Sugar Cookies

Every family has some kind of special homemade cookie that they eat only at Passover, so here is a version of the almond sugar cookies my mother used to make when I was a child. Instead of flour, we use ground almonds so that people on gluten-free diets can enjoy these light and delicious cookies too.

Yields 24 cookies

Ingredients

3 cups almonds, finely ground
   in a food processor

2 eggs
1 cup sugar

Procedure

Whisk the ingredients together until they are well combined.

Form into balls and place on baking trays.

Bake at 350° for 12 minutes.

SHAVUOT RECIPES

Many holidays have restrictions on what or where we are allowed to eat, but not Shavuot! Although eating dairy foods like blintzes and cheesecake is recommended, we also enjoy chicken soup, barbecued meats, and many other dishes. Shavuot is the holiday on which we can truly let our culinary prowess shine.

There are many reasons why it is customary to eat dairy products on the holiday of Shavout. Most importantly, on the day the Torah was given, we did not eat any meat. It is believed that the Torah was given on Shabbat, therefore on Shabbat it's forbidden to slaughter animals, so the Jewish people could not slaughter animals to have meat for the holiday itself. But other scholars believe the Jewish people did not eat meat that day because their vessels were not kosher, or because they had only recently learned about the laws of kashrut.

Another reason given for us eating dairy products on Shavout is that milk is a nurturing substance. Just as a baby begins life by drinking mother's milk, our eating dairy shows how the Torah nurtures us.

- Sweet Cheese Blintzes
- Lokshen Kugel
- Cheesecake

Sweet Cheese Blintzes

These blintzes provide a flavorful combination of cheese and sweetness—and they can easily be frozen and reheated for an easy breakfast treat.

Yields 10 to 13 blintzes

INGREDIENTS

4 oz. cream cheese

8 oz. farmer's cheese, strained

1 tablespoon vanilla

2 tablespoons brown sugar

1 egg

1 package regular crepe dough, defrosted

3 tablespoons oil for frying

Optional: Cinnamon for sprinkling

PROCEDURE

Mash the cream cheese, farmer's cheese, vanilla, brown sugar, and egg together with a fork; strain the filling with a fine mesh strainer.

Heat the oil in a pan for frying.

Meanwhile, place 2 tablespoons of filling in the center of each crepe and fold like an envelope: First fold the bottom halfway up, then fold the left and right sides in, and finally pull the top down.

Fry the blintzes in the oil on medium heat, turning each blintz after about two minutes until golden brown.

LOKSHEN KUGEL

In Yiddish, the word *kugel* comes from the German word for "sphere" and is also related to the traditional game *kugelach*, or "five stones," which is played similar to jacks. While German Jews baked their kugels in a round clay pot called a *kugeltopf,* today's kugels are baked in large square or rectangular pans.

There are several types of Kugel: savory, sweet, dairy, pareve (not containing meat or dairy products), potato, and noodle. Each kugel has its own story. On Shavuot, which celebrates he day the Torah was given on Mount Sinai, it's customary to eat dairy foods. Sweet, dairy-rich Lokshen Kugel is served because milk symbolizes the love and nurturing Torah gives us, and reminds us that Torah provides sustenance.

Yields 14 slices

INGREDIENTS

1 package wide egg noodles

2 cups sour cream

2 cups cottage cheese

1 teaspoon vanilla and ¾ cup sugar, combined to make vanilla sugar

3 eggs

1 teaspoon cinnamon

oil

¼ cup almond milk or coffee creamer

PROCEDURE

Preheat oven to 350°. Boil the egg noodles until mushy. Strain the water.

In a bowl, combine the cooked egg noodles with the cheeses, vanilla sugar, eggs, and milk or coffee creamer. Mix well.

Divide the mixture into two 9-inch round cake pans and sprinkle with half of the cinnamon. Coat evenly with a drizzle of oil.

Bake at 350° for 20 minutes or until golden brown.

Sprinkle with the remaining cinnamon before serving hot.

———∞———

Cheesecake

Traditionally, cheesecake is eaten on Shavuot to celebrate the giving of the Torah and to symbolize the land flowing with milk and honey. But many of us also enjoy cheesecake on special occasions year-round with our coffee.

Serves 12

Ingredients

¾ cup sugar

2 cups sour cream or cream cheese

2 cups farmer's cheese

1 tablespoon vanilla or maple syrup

2 tablespoons cornstarch

4 eggs

Procedure

Whip together the sugar, sour cream or cream cheese, farmer's cheese, vanilla or maple syrup, and corn starch until fluffy.

Add the eggs.

Pour the batter into a 12-inch spring-form cake pan. Place in a water bath (a larger pan filled with two inches of water).

Bake at 450° for 10 minutes. Lower temperature to 250° and bake for 1 hour.

Rosh Hashanah and Yom Kippur Recipes

When I was a child, the High Holidays—Rosh Hashanah, the Jewish New Year, and Yom Kippur, the Day of Atonement—made a great impression on me. I loved watching my grandfather sound the *shofar* on Rosh Hashanah and again at the end of Yom Kippur, and it moved me to see my father dressed in his kittel and the deep seriousness my grandparents and parents displayed. Best of all, we enjoyed many wonderful, symbolic foods together, and our meals, along with the great solemnity with which my family approached the holidays, kindled in me a deep desire to connect more closely to God.

- Honey Cake
- Merren Tzimmes
- Fruit Compote
- Apple Cake

HONEY CAKE

Honey cake is also known as *lekach*, which means "to take." On the eve of Yom Kippur, it is customary for the rebbe to hand out pieces of lekach before the fast begins, for eating it provides a blessing for a sweet new year. (Many families also serve lekach when breaking the fast at the end of Yom Kippur.) The idea is that if, in the upcoming year, you are, God forbid, destined to beg for food, this request can stand in its stead.

Serves 12

INGREDIENTS

4 eggs

2 cups raw honey

3 tablespoons oil

2 cups coffee, lukewarm

½ cup sugar

4 cups all-purpose flour

2 tablespoons baking powder

2 tablespoons baking soda

2 tablespoons nutmeg

PROCEDURE

Butter a 12-inch round cake pan or Bundt pan and set aside.

Mix the eggs, honey, oil, and coffee together, then add the dry ingredients and stir well.

Pour the batter into the cake pan and bake at 325° for 45 to 55 minutes until golden and an inserted knife comes out clean.

Merren Tzimmes

Traditionally, Tzimmes is a Jewish stew of sweetened vegetables, fruit and vegetables, or even meat with fruit and vegetables. I'm particularly fond of carrot Tzimmes. Carrots, in Yiddish, are called *merren*, which means "to increase." In Jewish tradition, names relate to a thing's essential qualities; for this reason, it's a time-honored custom to eat merren on Rosh Hashanah.

The very fact that merren connotes abundance makes it auspicious to eat carrots during the New Year, as it represents an increase in good things for the year to come.

Serves 7

Ingredients

8 carrots

1 cup fresh pineapple, diced into cubes

1 cup orange or pineapple juice

Pinch of ground nutmeg

Pinch of ground ginger

Pinch of cinnamon

3 tablespoons honey

Procedure

Remove the core of the pineapple and dice the fruit into cubes.

Peel and slice the carrots into ⅛-inch coins.

Combine the pineapple and carrots with the orange juice in a saucepan, then add the spices and honey to the pot.

Simmer, covered, for about 1 hour and 30 minutes, or until the carrots are cooked.

Serve hot.

Optional: To thicken, add 1 or 2 tablespoons of flour in the last 30 minutes of cooking. Also, 4 dried, pitted prunes may be diced and added, as well as 1 medium sweet potato, also diced.

Fruit Compote

This delicious dessert was actually invented out of necessity. Throughout history, eating apples out of season was impossible because there was no way to store them or transport them. People began cooking compote, the French word for applesauce, in order to extend apples' shelf life. Now, thanks to refrigeration and globalization, we can get apples—and any other kind of fruit, fresh or frozen—all year long. But compote is so delicious, healthy, and easy to cook, that it's still a popular dish to eat at the finish of a meal.

Serves 10

Ingredients

2 Granny Smith apples

2 MacIntosh apples

2 Honey Crisp or Fuji apples

1 cinnamon stick

1 cup grape juice

Procedure

Core, peel, and slice the apples and place them in a pot. Add the grape juice and cinnamon stick.

Cook on low, simmering for 2 hours and 30 minutes.

Remove the cinnamon stick and mash the apples.

Serve hot or cold.

To turn the applesauce into a genuine compote, add 10 large strawberries before cooking it. Wash them well, checking for insects. Remove their stems, and slice the strawberries in half. Sprinkle 2 tablespoons of sugar over the strawberries and macerate them for 20 minutes, then add the strawberries to the applesauce and simmer.

Apple Cake

As a young child I never ate apple cake, but when my sister started to cook, I tasted it for the first time and was hooked. Apples dipped in honey symbolize good wishes for a sweet, healthy New Year, and this recipe ensures a moist and flavorful cake.

Serves 12

Ingredients

Batter Ingredients

2½ cups all-purpose flour
1½ cups sugar
1 tablespoon cinnamon
1 teaspoon nutmeg
1 tablespoon baking powder
1 stick margarine, at room temperature
4 eggs

Filling

1 Granny Smith apple, 1 MacIntosh apple, and 1 Cortland apple, peeled and cut into ¼-inch slices
1 tablespoon cinnamon
2 tablespoons honey

Procedure

Prepare the apples and place them in a bowl. Sprinkle the cinnamon and drizzle the honey over the apples; mix well to coat thoroughly. Set aside.

Mix the batter's dry ingredients together, then add the margarine and eggs.

Butter and flour a Bundt pan and lay a row of apple slices over the bottom. Pour ⅓ of the batter evenly over the apples. Spread a layer of apples over the batter and then pour in another ⅓ of the batter. Lay the remaining apples and then pour the rest of the batter over them.

Bake at 350° for 25 minutes.

Sukkot and Simchat Torah Recipe

I find that the ambiance of sitting outdoors in the handmade sukkah for holiday meals during Sukkot enhances the food's flavors. Sukkot culminates in Simchat Torah, which celebrates our completing the public Torah readings and beginning them anew, and is a favorite holiday of mine. It reminds me of childhood and excites me about the future.

⸺⸺⸺

Holishkes (Stuffed Cabbage)

Stuffed cabbage, holishkes in Yiddish, is traditional in the Ukraine, Poland, and many Slavic countries. This recipe features seasoning from many different places, distinguishing it from other stuffed cabbage recipes. My family always served this dish on Simchat Torah. As a child, I noticed that two holishkes placed together resemble a Torah scroll.

Serve 1 stuffed cabbage per person

Ingredients

1 cup rice (uncooked if white, cooked if brown)
1 lb. ground meat or chicken
1 head of cabbage, cored

Sauce

28-oz. can tomato sauce
28-oz. can diced tomatoes
3 cloves garlic
½ cup of water

2 teaspoons salt
2 teaspoons black pepper
2 teaspoons dried basil
2 teaspoons garlic powder
¼ cup honey

Seasoning for meat

1 tablespoon ketchup
2 teaspoons garlic powder
1 teaspoon black pepper
1 teaspoon paprika

Place the cabbage in a 5-quart saucepan, covering it with water. Cover the saucepan and cook on low simmer until it comes to a boil. Boil for 20 minutes. Remove the cabbage from the water. After the cabbage cools, separate the leaves and remove the 10 largest leaves from the head. Rinse and check leaves for insects, and remove the vein from each leaf.

In a saucepan, combine tomato sauce, crushed tomatoes, spices, and garlic. Add honey and mix. Add water and put on low heat.

Combine the meat and white rice with the seasoning, then fill each of the 10 leaves with the mixture and wrap tightly.

Add to the sauce and cook on low heat for 1 hour.

Optional: Use layers of a large onion instead of cabbage leaves.

Chanukah Recipes

Chanukah is one of the best-known holidays on the Jewish calendar. The eight-day festival commemorates Jewish independence from the time of Greek occupation and the rededication of the Temple in Jerusalem, more than 2,000 years ago. During Chanukah, we remember that mankind's greatest purpose while on earth is to create light and dispel darkness.

It's customary to eat oily, fried foods in honor of the menorah in the Temple, which miraculously burned for eight days on only one day's worth of oil. Another tradition encourages eating dairy foods in honor of the heroism of Judith, who used salty cheese and wine to intoxicate and slay the Greek General Helipharnos, leaving his armies in disarray.

- Classic Potato Latkes
- Cheese Latkes
- Fruit Blintzes
- Sufganiyot (Jelly Donuts)

Latkes

In Eastern Europe, potatoes were a staple food, so to celebrate Chanukah the Ashkenazic Jews would grate and fry potatoes to make pancakes, or latkes. Today, latkes are synonymous with the holiday of Chanukah and can be flavored in a variety of ways.

CLASSIC POTATO LATKES

Serve 2 per person

INGREDIENTS

1 red potato, peeled

2 golden potatoes, peeled

1 small onion

1 egg

1 tablespoon salt

1 teaspoon black pepper

¼ cup oil for frying

1 tablespoon flour or gluten-free
ground flax seed, as binder

PROCEDURE

Grate coarsely the potatoes and onion. Mix in the other ingredients.

Pour ¼ cup oil into a frying pan on the stovetop on low heat. Scoop the mixture in the frying pan; flatten each scoop into a pancake. Fry each latke 3 minutes per side or until dark brown and crispy.

CHEESE LATKES

Serve 2 per person

INGREDIENTS

1 sweet potato, large

1 egg

½ cup cheddar, grated

A pinch of salt and pepper

oil for frying

1 tablespoon flour or gluten-free
ground flax seed, as binder

PROCEDURE

Grate the sweet potato into a bowl and mix it with cheddar cheese, egg, and flour or flax seed. Place ¼ cup oil in the frying pan and cook for 3 minutes on each side or until golden brown.

Fruit Blintzes

Blintzes, an old favorite of mine, are made of light, crepe-like dough. A good blintz should have a tasty filling. Here is the Chanukah blintz recipe that I find most flavorful.

Yields 8 to 10 blintzes

Ingredients

1 tablespoon maple syrup

1 cup blueberries

4 oz. goat cheese

8 oz. plain Greek yogurt or sour cream

2 tablespoons brown sugar

1 package regular crepe dough

3 tablespoons oil for frying

Procedure

Mash the blueberries, cheese, yogurt or sour cream, brown sugar, and maple syrup together with a fork; strain the filling with a fine mesh strainer.

Heat oil for frying in a pan.

Fill each crepe with two tablespoons of filling and wrap like an egg roll. Cook in oil until golden brown.

———⟨∞⟩———

SUFGANIYOT (JELLY DONUTS)

In the Middle East, the Sephardic Jews traditionally fried different forms of dough, which is where the *Sufganiyah*, a round jelly donut, comes from. Today, jelly donuts are a standard Chanukah treat. This recipe is easy and offers the greatest tasting jelly donuts my family has ever enjoyed.

Yields 16 donuts

INGREDIENTS

1 cup almond milk

1 tablespoon yeast

3½ cups all-purpose flour

2 eggs

3 tablespoons margarine

1 teaspoon kosher salt

1 tablespoon sugar

Oil for frying

Seedless jam, poured into a squirt bottle for filling

Powdered sugar for dusting

1 teaspoon lemon juice

PROCEDURE

Mix the yeast and almond milk in a bowl until it starts to puff up.

Place all of the dry ingredients in a mixer and knead. Then add the eggs, lemon juice, and the almond milk and yeast mixture to the dry ingredients and mix for 5 to 6 minutes until the dough is nice and supple.

Dust the countertop with flour. Roll the dough out onto the counter into a ½-inch-thick square; cover the dough with a towel and let it rise for 25 minutes. Use 2-inch round cookie cutters to cut out the donuts, then place them on a greased tray, cover with plastic wrap, and let them rise for 45 minutes.

Fry the donuts in a pan of oil, heated to about 375°, for about 3 minutes on each side or until golden brown.

Remove the donuts from the frying pan, and while they are still warm squirt jam into the center of each one. Dust the donuts with powdered sugar.

Tu B'Shevat Recipes

Each holiday brings up different childhood memories, and even as I prepare for Tu B'Shevat as an adult, I anticipate it with great excitement. On this holiday, we eat what are called the Seven Species of the Bible, a group of foods that grow in Israel and were traditionally offered in sacrifice at the Temple. The Arizal instituted the custom of having a Tu B'Shevat Seder, which many people still observe today.

- Pomegranate and Couscous Salad
- Fig Salad
- Cheese Salad

Pomegranate and Couscous Salad

Pomegranates and wheat are both praised in the Torah. I especially enjoy this salad because the combination of ingredients creates a delightful explosion of flavors.

Serves 5

Ingredients

2 cups Israeli, large-grained couscous, cooked
½ cup pomegranate seeds
¼ cup fresh parsley, chopped
Pinch of salt
Pinch of pepper

¼ cup pine nuts or slivered almonds
1 tablespoon lemon juice
1 tablespoon olive oil
1 teaspoon raw honey

Procedure

Mix the ingredients well with the couscous and serve immediately.

Cheese Salad

Israeli hotels serve amazing breakfast, and one morning on my first trip to Israel, I ate a cheese salad that I've never forgotten. I enjoyed it so much that when I came home, I created my own version, which brings back great memories every time I eat it. My family enjoys this dish at our meal celebrating Tu B'Shevat.

Serves 6

Ingredients

1 cup mozzarella cheese (fresh, if possible), cubed

½ red pepper diced

½ yellow pepper diced

3 scallions, chopped

Optional: 1 chili pepper, sliced thinly

Procedure

Toss the ingredients together into a bowl. Dress the salad with Yummy Pesto Butter on page 155 immediately before serving.

Fig Salad

Figs are native to Israel, and are praised in the Torah among the Seven Species. The buttery avocado, savory pistachios, and sharp onion really bring out the sweetness of the figs.

Serves 4

Ingredients

5 fresh figs, cut into slivers
1 avocado, cut into chunks
¼ cup chopped pistachios
½ purple onion, chopped finely

Dressing
2 tablespoons fresh-squeezed
  grapefruit
1 tablespoon honey
1 tablespoon fresh lime juice
1 tablespoon balsamic vinegar

Procedure

Toss the salad ingredients together in a bowl.

Mix the dressing ingredients and pour over the salad immediately before serving.

Purim Recipes

For the holiday of Purim, it's a mitzvah to be merry and to get intoxicated—but with spirituality, not spirits. When I was a child, wearing a costume to shul to hear the reading of the Megillah—the book of Esther—was the most fun of the entire year.

- Kreplach
- Hamantaschen

Kreplach (Dumplings)

These "Jewish wontons" are eaten as appetizers or in soup on Purim, Yom Kippur, and the last day of Sukkot. Usually stuffed with ground meat, they can be made with homemade pasta dough or wonton wrappers.

Serve 1 per person

Ingredients

1 cup ground meat	1 teaspoon paprika
1 small onion, grated	1 teaspoon cumin
1 teaspoon salt	1 egg
1 teaspoon black pepper	2 quarts chicken broth
1 teaspoon garlic powder	

Procedure

Mix the filling ingredients together in a bowl and set aside.

Place 1 tablespoon of the filling in the center of each wonton square and fold it diagonally; then fold the ends over together so the dumpling looks like an envelope.

Heat the chicken broth to boiling. Place the kreplach into broth and continue boiling for 4 minutes.

Hamantaschen

There are many different stories about why we eat Hamantaschen, three-cornered cookies, on the holiday of Purim, which celebrates the victory of the Jewish people over the villain Haman's decree that all Jewish people—men, women, and children—should be destroyed in a single day.

Some people believe that the cookies got their shape from Haman's pocket, which was filled with money that he offered in exchange for permission to kill all Jews, or which held the ancient dice used to determine which day was best to begin his onslaught. Others believe that the cookies are modeled after Haman's three-cornered hat.

Regardless of how the cookie got its shape, there is a deeper reason for eating Hamantaschen. In Judaism, there are two types of miracles: the kind that defies the laws of nature, like the oil lamps burning for eight nights at Chanukah, and the kind that works within nature, like the miracle of Purim. Of the two types of miracles, the miracle that occurs within nature is far greater and on a higher natural and spiritual plane than a miracle in which nature is altered and changed.

To symbolize Purim's great miracle, which occurred in nature, we give Hamantaschen a sweet filling. Hamantaschen may look like ordinary cookies, but when we bite into one, we discover a tasty mystery hidden inside. In the same way, nature may not appear extraordinary on the surface, but if we look deeply into it, we discover its secret miracles.

Yields about 18 cookies

Ingredients

3 cups all-purpose flour

1 cup sugar

1½ sticks margarine or butter

1 tablespoon baking soda

2 teaspoons orange juice concentrate
  or orange zest

2 eggs

¼ cup sugar crystals

½ cup jam, any flavor

1 tablespoon cornstarch

Egg wash: 1 egg mixed with 1 teaspoon water

Preheat the oven at 350°.

Mix together in a food processor: flour, sugar, margarine or butter, baking soda, orange juice or zest, and eggs. Cover the dough with plastic wrap and refrigerate it for 1 hour.

Spread plastic wrap on a countertop or table and place the dough on it. Cover the dough with plastic wrap and use a rolling pin to roll the dough out to ⅛ inch or ¼ inch, depending on the desired thickness.

Use a 3-inch cookie cutter to cut perfectly round circles of dough. Put a teaspoon of filling in the center of each circle. Using egg wash on the edges as a sealer, fold in the sides of the circle to make triangle, with the corner of each side overlapping the next side.

Egg wash the Hamantaschen and sprinkle them with sugar crystals. Bake for 6 minutes or until light brown.

Breakfast Dishes

After we awaken and greet the day with prayer, we fortify ourselves for the activities that lie ahead. In a family, breakfast is also the first time we gather together and provides a moment of closeness before we all head off to fulfill our purposes. We may not always have time to prepare special dishes for the first meal of the day, but whenever we can, why not make breakfast delightful?

- Shakshuka
- Challah French Toast
- Montreal-Style Bagels
- Gravlax
- Matzah Brei

Shakshuka

Shakshuka is made with matbucha (see recipe on page 210) and can be eaten for breakfast or lunch. As such, it's an especially versatile dish, various versions of which are becoming a staple at hip restaurants in Brooklyn.

Ingredients

Approximately 1 cup or more Matbucha

4 eggs

Procedure

Using a spoon, spread matbucha flat into the frying pan. Crack the eggs over the dip but do not mix them into it. Let the ingredients cook over low heat for 20 minutes. Serve hot.

CHALLAH FRENCH TOAST

In the Torah, the concept of *bal tashchit*, not wasting anything, applied to many aspects of life, but it is especially important when it comes to food. After the holy Shabbat day, we often have extra challah, and there's no better way to use it than to turn it into French toast for a delicious Sunday morning breakfast. (Make sure the challah has not come in contact with any meat.)

Serves 6

INGREDIENTS

6 slices of challah (about 1½ inches thick)

1 cup milk

2 eggs

1 teaspoon cinnamon

Pinch of nutmeg

PROCEDURE

Slice the challah into 1½-inch slices.

Mix the batter and dunk the challah slices into it one at a time, coating each one well with batter.

Allow the challah to sit for 20 minutes to absorb the batter until nice and soggy.

Fry each slice in an oiled skillet at medium to high heat for 1 minute per side or until golden brown.

Montreal-Style Bagels

Although bagels are identified with the cultures of New York City and Montreal, the truth is that the bagel originated in Eastern Europe. The Jewish bakers in the shtetls, primarily in Poland, all had their own methods of bagel-making, and when they emigrated from Eastern Europe to Montreal or New York, they brought their signature styles of bagels with them.

Yields 1 dozen

Ingredients

Dough

1½ cups water at room temperature

2 tablespoons dry, quick-rising yeast

1 egg

¼ cup oil

½ cup honey

5 cups bread flour

1 tablespoon kosher salt

4 quarts boiling water

⅓ cup honey

1 tablespoon baking soda

Pinch of kosher salt, sesame seeds, and poppy seeds, mixed together for topping

Have on hand

Water in spray bottle

Procedure

In a measuring cup, mix together the water, yeast, and honey and pour into the mixing bowl of a Kitchen Aid or equivalent that has a dough hook.

Stir in the whole eggs, and oil. Mix well.

Add the flour and salt, and mix until the dough forms a soft, flexible dough, about 6 to 9 minutes. If the dough seems too wet, add a bit more flour. Once mixed properly, no dough will stick to the walls of the mixing bowl.

When the dough is smooth and elastic, place it on a lightly floured work space and divide into 3½-oz. portions. Allow the portions to rest for about 20 minutes on the counter with a plastic wrap covering.

Preheat the oven to 450° with a pizza stone.

Shape the portions into bagels by rolling each piece to an 8-inch coil. Fold the ends over each other, pressing with the palm of one hand and rolling back and forth until two ends unite into one. Make sure this connects the ends together properly or the bagels will open while boiling them. Let the bagels rise for 30 minutes on a sheet tray sprayed with non-stick spray.

Put the topping mix in a bowl and set aside.

Meanwhile, bring the 4 quarts of water and ¹/₃ cup of honey to a boil in a pot big enough to fit 3 or 4 bagels.

When the water comes to a boil, add 1 tablespoon of baking soda. Expect a bubbling or fizzing effect.

While the water is boiling, add 3 bagels to the water with a wire spider. Boil for 40 seconds and flip each one to their opposite side. Boil for another 40 seconds and remove from the water.

Sprinkle both sides of the boiled bagels with the seed mixture and immediately place on the stone in the oven. Spray once with water and bake for approximately 15 minutes, or until the bagels develop a golden-brown color.

Gravlax

A lot of kosher food is not necessarily connected to anything spiritual or holy. Some dishes are culturally based. As a people, the Jews have traveled the world and learned the cuisine of many locales; because of this, foods like lox are considered kosher.

Serve 4 slices per person (leftovers can be wrapped and frozen)

Ingredients

½ cup salt

½ cup brown sugar

1 side of fresh salmon (about 2 to 4 pounds), with skin

Topping

¼ bunch of fresh dill, finely chopped

1 tablespoon maple syrup

1 tablespoon black pepper

Have on hand

Plastic wrap

A brick or heavy pot

Procedure

Cut the side of salmon in half width-wise, and wash the pieces well.

Combine the salt and sugar and coat both sides of each piece of fish with the mixture.

Place one piece of salmon flesh-side on top of the other, so that the skins are on the outside and the flesh is sandwiched. Wrap the salmon tightly in plastic wrap and puncture holes in the plastic wrap to allow the juices to drain as needed.

Place the wrapped salmon on a tray and place a brick or heavy pot on top to act as a weight. Refrigerate the weighted salmon for 24 hours.

Flip the salmon over, replace the weight, and refrigerate for an additional 24 hours.

Remove the weight and unwrap the fish. Rinse off the salt mixture. Pat the salmon dry.

Coat half of the salmon with chopped dill and rewrap in plastic wrap. Refrigerate for 12 hours.

Coat the other half of the salmon with maple syrup. Sprinkle black pepper over the salmon and rewrap in plastic wrap. Refrigerate for 12 hours.

Once the salmon has marinated for 12 hours, it is ready to be sliced and served.

MATZAH BREI

There are many myths about the origin of pizza and its connection to the round matzah. So too some people say that French toast was invented as a copy of Matzah Brei. Either way, what better way to eat matzah during the week of Passover!

Serves 2

INGREDIENTS

1 shmurah (round) matzah or 2 regular (square) matzahs

2 eggs

¼ cup whole milk

1 teaspoon cinnamon

1 teaspoon vanilla

1 teaspoon sugar

PROCEDURE

Run the matzah(s) under cold water and break them into pieces, placing them into a bowl.

In another bowl, mix together the eggs, milk, sugar, vanilla, and cinnamon.

Toss the matzah(s) into the mixture and let stand 10 minutes.

Fry the matzah(s) on high heat, stirring the mixture as you would scramble eggs. Serve immediately.

Dips and Salads

If you ask a Jewish person to name a food that isn't kosher and is therefore forbidden to eat, the first response is usually pork. Although that is correct, there are other foods that are even more gravely forbidden to eat. One of those foods is insects. When you eat a complete insect, you violate as many as six or seven prohibitions, while if you eat pig, you only violate one.

All produce has an infestation of insects, many of which are tiny and hard to see. Insects in produce is even more prevalent today as we move away from the use of pesticides. Organic farming is certainly healthier, but it increases the chance of infestation, especially for someone like myself with a home garden, so it's even more important, when using produce for salads, to wash the produce thoroughly and have a system in place to check that there is no known infestation of insects.

Here are some of my daughters' favorite dips and salads, which we enjoy year-round, but especially in the summer when our garden is abundant with fresh ingredients.

Dips:

- Hummus
- Matbucha (Moroccan Tomato Dip)
- Tahini Dip

Salads:

- Beet and Arugula Salad
- Coleslaw
- Cucumber Salad
- Garden Salad with Ginger Dressing
- Israeli Salad
- Lemon Pepper Carrot Salad
- Potato Salad

Dips

———— ✦ ————

Hummus

Although fresh or dried chickpeas can be used to make a superior-tasting hummus, it's quicker and easier to use canned chickpeas. I find them more readily available, and my family prefers them, too.

Ingredients

16-ounce can of chickpeas, drained
2 tablespoons tahini paste
1 teaspoon lemon juice
1 teaspoon salt
2 tablespoons olive oil

For serving

1 teaspoon paprika
1 teaspoon olive oil

Procedure

Grind the ingredients together in a blender until smooth or the desired consistency. (Personally, I like hummus to be a bit chunky.)

Pour the mixture neatly into a circle on a plate. With a spoon, carve out the center to create a small bowl. Pour in the additional olive oil and top with paprika.

Serve with pita slices (see recipe for Pita Bread on page 230).

———— ✦ ————

Matbucha (Moroccan Tomato Dip)

In Jewish homes throughout the Middle East, Matbucha is typically found on the Shabbat table, and Syrian and Turkish Jews serve similar dips. It also makes a delicious addition to fried eggs for breakfast (or lunch); see recipe for Shakshuka on page 203.

Ingredients

5 cloves of garlic

5 ripe vine tomatoes

1 jalapeño sliced into thin circles

½ red pepper, julienned

1 tablespoon salt

1 teaspoon garlic powder

Pinch of cumin

Pinch of black pepper

¼ cup oil for frying

Procedure

Pour the oil into a saucepan. Add the garlic and cook until translucent.

Add the tomatoes, peppers, and spices and let them simmer, covered, on low heat for 2 hours. Cool before serving.

—⊶⊷—

TAHINI DIP

It's possible to make your own tahini paste from ground sesame seeds, but I don't think it's worth the effort. This recipe includes commercially prepared tahini paste, available from any grocer.

INGREDIENTS

4 tablespoons tahini paste

1 tablespoon lemon juice

4 tablespoons water

4 stalks cilantro, chopped finely

1 tablespoon salt

1 teaspoon paprika

1 teaspoon black pepper

PROCEDURE

Mix the ingredients in a jar, put the lid on, and shake the jar well for about 3 minutes.

Serve with cut vegetables or in a pita with falafel.

Salads

—◦◦◦—

Beet and Arugula Salad

When it comes to salads, I am a minimalist. I do not like heavy dressing because I like the ingredients to stand out on their own. Less is more. I love this salad especially because I grow these ingredients in my garden.

Serves 6

Ingredients

10 oz. baby spinach
10 oz. arugula
1 small red beet
1 small yellow beet, sliced
½ red onion
1 tablespoon grated ginger

Dressing

2 tablespoons honey
⅓ cup sesame oil or extra virgin olive oil
⅓ cup fresh lime juice
½ teaspoon salt
¼ teaspoon pepper, freshly ground

Procedure

Boil fresh beets in water until tender. Do not use canned beets, which have high levels of sodium and are preseasoned.

Once the beets are cooked and drained, peel and slice them. Combine them with the rest of the ingredients.

Mix the dressing in a separate bowl. Add the dressing to the salad and toss until incorporated.

—◦◦◦—

Coleslaw

When I was growing up, my family only ate sauerkraut with hot dogs. Today, there is a wide array of condiments for hot dogs as well as for hamburgers, or even for use as side dishes. My personal favorite for both is coleslaw, which I believe takes sauerkraut to the next level.

Serves 8

Ingredients

½ head of cabbage

1 carrot

¼ cup lemon juice

¼ cup pineapple juice

½ cup sugar

½ cup mayonnaise

Procedure

Shred the cabbage using a slicer blade.

Shred the carrots using a grater blade. Place the cabbage and carrots into a bowl.

Add in the remaining ingredients and mix well. Wait 30 minutes and mix again.

Serve cold. Coleslaw may be refrigerated for up to 3 days before serving.

Cucumber Salad

My uncle, Rabbi S. B. Hecht, is the chief Sephardic rabbi of Queens in New York City, and in 1979 he played a major role in Operation Exodus, the Chabad rescue of 1,800 Iranian Jewish children during the Iranian Revolution. When I was a child and would visit his synagogue, the Persian cook who worked there always made this salad, and it is truly a delight.

Serves 6

Ingredients

1 tablespoon salt

1 teaspoon pepper, freshly ground

2 English cucumbers, peeled or unpeeled, thinly sliced

⅓ cup lemon juice or 2 fresh lemons

2 to 3 tablespoons sugar

⅛ bunch of dill, finely chopped

½ red onion, thinly sliced or finely diced

Procedure

Slice the cucumbers and red onion thinly or dice them finely, as preferred, and combine them in a bowl.

Chop the dill finely and add it to the sliced cucumbers and onion.

Mix well together the spices, sugar, and lemon juice, and add it to the salad.

Toss well and set aside to settle for 30 minutes in the refrigerator. Toss again just before serving chilled.

Garden Salad with Ginger Dressing

I am blessed to live in a small village in a home with 1¹/₂ acres of land, which allows me to have a nice-sized garden. From late spring through early fall, I can go out and pick produce to use in salads. When I work in the garden, I think about the many Chassidic rebbes who encouraged their Chassidim to move to small villages and start farming communes to sustain themselves and their families. This way of life allowed them to be free to practice and serve God in the way they saw fit without the distractions of busy city life.

Serves 5

Ingredients

1 head of romaine lettuce or mixed
   greens
1 vine tomato
1 house cucumber
1 scallion

Dressing

1 teaspoon fresh ginger, peeled and
   sliced very fine or grated (Hint:
   The best way to peel ginger is
   with a spoon.)
1 teaspoon soy sauce
1 tablespoon sesame oil
1 tablespoon honey

Procedure

After properly washing, checking, and chopping the lettuce, dice the tomatoes and cucumbers, and slice the scallions all finely and place everything in a salad bowl.

Add the dressing and toss, mixing well.

Israeli Salad

Many of the foods we love best are the ones that take us back to our childhood. But another way to experience food is by celebrating with it and enjoying it with our children.

Selling vegetables to your children can be a very hard thing, especially in America, where there's a lot of junk food competing with the healthy foods. Children often don't like salad, especially when it's served in a large bowl and contains a lot of lettuce or many vegetables with a bitter taste. Israeli Salad is a great way to get kids used to eating salad because it's made of several tasty vegetables, finely chopped. I have introduced each of my kids to vegetables by serving them Israeli Salad, and they are always excited and happy to eat it.

Serves 4

Ingredients

½ red pepper

1 house cucumber

2 tomatoes

½ red onion

¼ bunch of cilantro

¼ cup lemon juice

3 tablespoons olive oil

1 teaspoon kosher salt

Pinch of black pepper

Procedure

Dice all the vegetables finely. Chop the cilantro finely. Mix in the oil, spices, and lemon juice. Toss and serve.

LEMON PEPPER CARROT SALAD

This recipe will turn any carrot-salad skeptic into a fan. It can be served with a meat or fish course, and is a childhood favorite of mine that's sure to knock your socks off as well. Very refreshing!

Serves 6

INGREDIENTS

8 medium carrots, peeled

4 scallions, finely chopped

¼ cup sugar (optional)

½ cup lemon juice from 2 to 3 fresh lemons

1 tablespoon olive oil

Pinch of sea salt

½ teaspoon black pepper, freshly ground

½ teaspoon garlic powder

4 tablespoons water

PROCEDURE

Grate the carrots using the grater's larger setting.

In a bowl, add the grated carrots, chopped scallions, sugar, lemon juice, olive oil, salt, pepper, and garlic powder.

Mix until incorporated.

Let sit in its juices for 1 hour before serving chilled.

Optional: For an extra kick, finely slice up and add half a jalapeño pepper.

Potato Salad

In Ashkenazi homes, potato salad is a staple, so there are many different recipes available for this traditional dish. Usually, however, the recipe that people use is the one that was passed down from their grandmother. Here is my own bubbe's recipe.

Serves 7

Ingredients

5 to 6 large red potatoes
2 scallions, chopped finely
¼ cup red onion, chopped finely
⅓ cup olive oil
½ teaspoon black pepper

1 teaspoon garlic powder
¼ cup red pepper, finely sliced
1 teaspoon salt
1 teaspoon brown mustard
Optional: 2 tablespoons
    mayonnaise

Procedure

Boil potatoes with the skin on.

Dice the potatoes after they have cooled.

Combine the ingredients in a bowl and toss. Serve at room temperature.

Optional: Add 2 tablespoons of mayonnaise before tossing.

Desserts

My family always enjoys capping off dinner with dessert. Having children help out with preparing dessert is a great way to teach them their way around the kitchen.

- Dessert Tzimmes
- Rugelach
- Easy Single-Layer Napoleons

Dessert Tzimmes

I was thrilled to compete on the Food Network's hit show *Chopped*. As a finalist, in just 30 minutes I turned traditional Tzimmes into a sweet dessert, and wowed the judges!

Serves 8

Ingredients

1 bunch rainbow carrots (approximately eight)

2 cups simple syrup (equal parts water and sugar, brought to a boil)

8 fresh figs

2 tablespoons margarine or butter

1 tablespoon brown sugar

Procedure

Peel the carrots and boil them in simple syrup until tender.

Slice the figs in half and place in a pan with the cut side facing down. Caramelize for 3 minutes on medium heat. Once the figs are tender, slice the carrots and add them to the figs.

Add the margarine or butter and sprinkle with brown sugar.

Candy the carrots for about 4 minutes, and serve warm.

Rugelach

Every cuisine features its own distinctive pastries, and, in my opinion, the number one pastry of Ashkenazic and Sephardic Jewish cooking is the rugelach. Made by wrapping a triangle of dough around a filling, the rugelach is similar to a croissant, but cookie-sized and with a thicker texture.

There are many stories about the origin of this pastry. Some say the word *rugelach* means "twisted," and refers to the pastry's shape. The rugelach is so popular today that it is considered the quintessential kosher Jewish pastry. There are many versions, along with a seemingly endless variety of rugelach fillings, including fruits like cherry, apricot, and raspberry; cream cheese; and even chocolate.

Yields 32 pastries

Ingredients

Dough

½ cup (4 oz.) non-dairy cream cheese, softened
2 cups margarine, softened
3 cups all-purpose flour or cake flour
Pinch of salt
1 tablespoon vanilla or maple syrup

Topping

Egg wash: 1 egg mixed with 1 teaspoon water
1 teaspoon sugar, for dusting

Filling

¼ cup jam of your choice
⅛ cup pecans, roughly chopped
⅛ cup pistachios, roughly chopped
½ teaspoon cinnamon
¼ teaspoon maple syrup

Preheat oven to 350°. Mix the room-temperature cream cheese and margarine in a bowl, using an electric mixer, until combined.

Slowly add the flour and salt, and mix until it forms dough. Add a tablespoon of either vanilla extract or maple syrup for added flavor, according to your liking.

Wrap dough in plastic wrap and refrigerate for 45 minutes. If the dough is not firm and cold, refrigerate for an additional 15 to 20 minutes.

For the filling, combine the jam, chopped nuts, cinnamon, and maple syrup in a small bowl.

When the dough is cold, remove plastic wrap and cut the dough in quarters to create a more manageable piece to roll. Dust the counter with flour to prevent the dough from sticking as you roll. Roll the dough to ⅛ inch thick. Use an 8-inch circle to cut the dough to size. Remove the excess. Spread the filling evenly over the circle.

Cut the circle into 8 symmetrical pieces as you would cut a pizza or pie.

Starting from the widest end of the triangle, roll in an upward direction toward to the smallest end.

Align the rugelach on a sheet tray lined with parchment paper, leaving room in between each piece for expansion, brush the tops with egg wash, and sprinkle with sugar before placing in the oven.

Bake for 20 minutes, or until the dough is evenly baked.

Easy Single-Layer Napoleons

Traditionally, Napoleons have a few layers, but our family enjoys this simple, single-layer version, which my children enjoy making themselves for Shabbat dinner.

Serve 1 square per person

Ingredients

17.3-oz. package puff pastry sheets

10 strawberries, sliced lengthwise

Filling

1 cup nondairy creamer

1 tablespoon vanilla pudding powder

Topping

½ cup confectioner's sugar

2 tablespoons water

Procedure

Combine nondairy creamer with vanilla pudding powder, using a mixer. Whip until firm.

Split puff pastry in half and lay half on a baking sheet.

Spread the filling over the pastry and layer the filling with the sliced strawberries.

Lay the other half of the puff pastry over the strawberries.

Whisk together the confectioner's sugar and water, and pour it over the top.

Chill for at least 3 hours. Cut into squares for serving.

Year-Round Family Favorites

For dinner during the week, and for community meals on Shabbat, when I am hosting many people with diverse tastes I like to fall back on some of my old favorites, some of which have Middle-Eastern origins.

- Kosher Pickles
- Knishes
- Cheese Bourekas
- Falafel
- S'chug
- Pita Bread

Kosher Pickles

Pickles are amazingly easy to prepare and make a refreshing side dish at any meal.

Yields 6 pickles

Ingredients

6 small Persian cucumbers
½ hot pepper
1 tablespoon pickle spice blend
4 cloves garlic
4 stalks dill

Brine

2 tablespoons salt
4 cups water

Procedure

Combine the salt and water to create the brine.

Add the spices, cucumbers, garlic, and dill.

Let sit for 48 hours in the refrigerator.

Serve chilled.

Knishes

There are many ways of making knishes, which hail from the Eastern Europe diaspora. Some people bake them, others fry them. Traditionally, knishes are made with a flaky dough similar to strudel which requires a great deal of time to prepare, but my recipe for knishes uses a simple and easy way to make puff pastry dough.

Yields 10 knishes

Ingredients

Dough	*Filling*
2 cups flour	2 rustic potatoes
1 tablespoon baking soda	1 large white onion, diced
Pinch of salt	1 tablespoon salt
2 sticks butter (or margarine)	1 teaspoon black pepper
⅔ cup ice cold water	2 tablespoons oil

Egg Wash

1 egg mixed with 1 teaspoon water

Procedure

First make the filling:

In a large skillet, fry the onion in oil, stirring often; when translucent, add salt and pepper, continuing stirring until fried golden brown.

Peel and dice the potatoes and place in a 3-quart pot with enough water to cover them. Boil the potatoes on medium heat until soft.

Drain the potatoes of 90 percent of the water. Add the fried onions and $^1/_2$ stick butter or margarine. Mash until a very smooth consistency, add salt and pepper to taste.

Next make the dough:

Preheat the oven to 375°.

Grease a baking tray with butter or margarine and set aside.

Prepare the egg wash and set aside.

Blend together the dry ingredients.

Add half a stick of butter to the flour and crumble loosely together with your hand.

Add the cold water and knead for about 6 minutes until the dough is nice and elastic. If the dough is too dry, add a tablespoon of water at a time. (The weather and the amount of moisture in the air can affect dough formation.)

Roll out the dough into a rectangle about $1/8$ inch thick and let it rest on the counter for 10 minutes.

While the dough is resting, cut the remaining 1½ stick of butter into pieces lengthwise. Lay the strips of butter out on parchment paper and place them in the freezer for 5 minutes.

After the strips of butter have chilled, place them on top of the dough and use a rolling pin to blend the butter into the dough.

Fold the dough over three times, like a brochure. Place a sheet of parchment paper over the dough and roll the dough out into rectangle again. Place the dough into the freezer and allow it to rest for 5 minutes.

Repeat the folding, freezing, and rolling steps 3 times, letting the dough rest 10 minutes in between, and *voila*! Your knish dough is ready. (Traditional recipes call for the dough to rest in the refrigerator for 30 minutes between rolls.)

Roll out the dough to $1/8$-inch thickness and cut into 4 x 4-inch squares. Place a generous tablespoon of the mixture into the center of each square. Fold its 4 corners in, followed by its sides. Pinch the top closed and press down until you have a nice circle shape.

Brush the top of each knish with egg wash.

Place the knishes on a greased baking tray and bake for 30 minutes or until golden.

CHEESE BOUREKAS

Although the *boureka*—a small, savory hand pie—is not a Jewish food, it is traditional in some of the countries where Jews lived during the diaspora. This includes Turkey, where the boureka is said to have originated, as well as the Middle East, North Africa, and parts of Asia. Iberian Jews are said to have included bourekas in their Shabbat meals as far back as the sixteenth century. In Israel today, bourekas are a staple, served as street food and for breakfast, and there is no bakery that doesn't offer them. Bourekas come with a wide variety of fillings, including cheese, beef, potatoes, mushrooms, spinach, and eggplant, and they are often sprinkled with sesame seeds.

My favorite is cheese bourekas. Although I prefer to use feta cheese made from sheep's milk mixed with ricotta cheese, you can also substitute other cheeses according to your liking.

Yields 12 bourekas

INGREDIENTS

2 sheets puff pastry, defrosted

Filling

½ cup feta cheese, made from sheep's milk
½ cup ricotta
¼ cup fresh parsley, chopped finely
1 egg

Egg Wash

1 egg mixed with 1 teaspoon water

Topping

½ cup sesame seeds, for sprinkling
Parmesan cheese, freshly grated,
    for sprinkling (optional)

Preheat oven to 375° and line a tray with parchment paper.

Mix filling together using a fork until smooth consistency.

Cut the defrosted puff pastry into 3 x 3-inch squares and fill each one with 2 heaping tablespoons of cheese mixture.

Fold the filled pastry squares into triangles, using a fork to press down the sides and seal them.

Brush with egg wash and sprinkle with sesame seeds and parmesan cheese.

Bake for 14 minutes or until golden brown.

Falafel

Jewish foods are often influenced by the many countries in which Jews have lived throughout the 2,000 years of the diaspora, and falafel is a great example of this. Since many Middle Eastern cuisines feature fried legumes, it's not surprising that in Israel, where people from all over the world live together, falafel is the most popular street food. For instance, falafel is served in a pita, which comes from the Mediterranean and Turkey, as well as in a *laffah*, which comes from Syria. Falafel is also often served with a spicy relish called *s'chug*, which originated with Yemenite Jews.

Yields 18 falafel balls

Ingredients

1 cup raw chickpeas, soaked overnight in a cool area	Challah breadcrumbs or regular breadcrumbs
1 tablespoon olive oil	1 egg
3 heads of scallions	1 teaspoon salt
½ bunch cilantro	Pinch of black pepper
½ jalapeño pepper	1 tablespoon tahini
½ white onion	Oil for deep frying

Procedure

Once the chickpeas are finished soaking, dry them and grind them very finely in the blender, slowly pouring in the olive oil until they form a chunky paste.

Remove the chickpea paste from the blender and place it in a large mixing bowl.

Grind the cilantro, scallions, onion, and jalapeño in the blender until they form a very fine paste.

Combine the two pastes together in a bowl. Add the challah (or bread) crumbs, egg, spices, salt, pepper, and tahini, and mix well. Cover the bowl and let it sit in the refrigerator for 30 minutes. After chilling, form the falafel mixture into golf ball-sized balls.

Heat oil in the deep fryer to 365°. Deep fry the falafel balls for 1 minute each or until golden brown.

S'CHUG

This spicy relish is not common in America, but in Israel it's a very popular condiment for street falafel.

INGREDIENTS

½ bunch Italian parsley, chopped
3 cloves garlic
1 jalapeño pepper

1 chili pepper
¼ cup olive oil
salt to taste

PROCEDURE

Combine the ingredients in a food processor and grind until smooth.

S'chug will keep in the refrigerator for 2 weeks if stored properly.

Pita Bread

In my opinion, pita is the best bread for a sandwich. With a hamburger bun, or even regular bread, a sandwich's fillings can spill out. But pita holds all of the ingredients in its pocket, allowing every bite to be savored without making a mess.

Yields 10 pitas

Ingredients

2½ cups bread flour

2 cups warm water

1½ tablespoons yeast

1 tablespoon olive oil

1 teaspoon honey

1 tablespoon kosher salt

Flour for dusting

Procedure

Put the honey, yeast, and half the water into a mixing bowl and mix lightly with a fork. Allow the mixture to sit until it becomes bubbly. Add the flour, salt, olive oil, and remaining water and mix with a dough hook on low speed for 2 minutes and then on medium speed for 5 minutes.

The dough should be sticky, but if it is too sticky, add ¼ cup of flour.

Allow the dough to rise for 2 hours.

Meanwhile, after 1½ hours of letting the dough rise, turn the oven onto its highest setting for 30 minutes for preheating. When the oven is ready, place a metal tray upside down on the bottom rack.

Form the dough into 1.5-oz. balls. Using dusting flour, form the balls into flat ¼-inch-thick coins.

Cover the small loaves with a towel and let them rise for 10 more minutes. Then place them on the preheated tray in the oven and bake at for 2 to 3 minutes, or just until the pita begins puffing up.

Recipes Index

A Glossary of Jewish
and Chassidic Terms

Chabad: Sometimes referred to as Chabad-Lubavitch, this orthodox Jewish Chassidic movement was founded by Rabbi Schneur Zalman of Liadi in the Russian village of Lubavitch in 1775. In 1951, Rabbi Menachem Mendel Schneerson became the seventh Chabad (Lubavitcher) Rebbe and transformed Chabad into one of the largest Jewish movements in the world. Chabad is characterized by its demand for intellectual development as well as its emphasis on the performance of mitzvot, good deeds honoring God and acts of kindness toward other people.

Chassid: Someone who goes beyond the letter of Jewish Law, a follower of Chassidism.

Chassidic Chagas: The original form of Chassidism, as taught by the Ba'al Shem Tov, previous to the development of Chabad.

Chevraya Kadisha: The Holy Society, or inner circle of followers, founded by the Maggid Rebbe Dov Ber of Mezeritch (second leader of the Chabad Hasidic movement).

Chofetz Chaim: A nickname for the Torah scholar and Jewish leader Rabbi Yisrael Meir Kagan (1838–1933), the author of *Chafetz Chaim*, a work establishing the guidelines of proper speech.

Farbrengen: A joyous Chabad-Lubavitch Chassidic gathering, also called a "tish" by other Chassidic groups, which is led by a rebbe and features discussion of the Torah and Chassidic philosophy, storytelling, singing, and refreshments. A farbrengen is considered a very holy time.

Halachic: Pertaining to Jewish law.

HaMotzi: The blessing over the covered challah bread, which begins the Shabbat meal, traditionally said in Hebrew, translates as: "Blessed are You, Adonai our God, Ruler of the Universe, who brings forth bread from the earth."

Hoshanna Rabbah: The seventh day of Sukkot.

Klipot: Shells, or coverings of impurity, created by a person's negative actions that create a mystical barrier to God.

Menachem Mendel Schneerson: A rabbi (1902–1994) and the seventh Lubavitcher Rebbe, who was widely considered one of the most influential Jewish leaders of the twentieth century.

Mishnah: The first written version of the Jewish oral traditions and the first section of the Talmud, also considered the first major work of rabbinic literature.

OBM: Of blessed memory.

Perkei Avot: The Hebrew name of *Chapters of Our Fathers*, a compilation of traditional Jewish ethical teachings composed during the early Rabbinic Period.

Pesach: The Hebrew name for the holiday of Passover.

Rebbetzin: A rabbi's wife.

Rosh Chodesh: The first day of the Jewish month.

Saba Kadisha: Solomon Eliezer Alfandari (1826–1930), a distinguished Kabbalist and rabbi who held many important leadership roles, including Chief Rabbi of Damascus and Safed.

Sefer Yetzirah: The Hebrew name for The Book of Creation (or Formation), the earliest extant book on Jewish mysticism, which is said to contain the secrets to Creation.

Sefirot: The modes or attributes through which God manifests Himself.

Shmuel Munkes: Perhaps the most famous follower of the Rebbe Shneur Zalman of Liadi, who was known for his wit and "Chassidic pranks."

Shneur Zalman of Liadi: The rabbi who founded Chabad and became its first Rebbe; he lived from 1745 to 1812 and was the author of many books, including The Tanya.

Sukkah: A temporary hut built and used for gathering for meals during the holiday of Sukkot. The sukkah represents the dwellings in which the Israelites lived during their forty years of wandering in the desert.

Talmud: An extensive collection of writings about Jewish law and tradition compiled and edited by rabbis between the third and sixth centuries, the Talmud has two components: the *Mishnah*, a written compendium of Jewish Oral Torah; and the *Gemara*, an elucidation of the Mishnah, which also expounds broadly on the Hebrew Bible.

Tanya: An early work of Chassidic philosophy written by Chabad Chassidism's founder, Rabbi Shneur Zalman of Liadi and published in 1797.

Torah: A range of meanings is ascribed to Torah; most commonly, Torah refers to the law of God as revealed to Moses and recorded in the first five books of the Hebrew scriptures, the *Pentateuch*.

Torah also refers to the entire Jewish Bible, which contains the full twenty-four books of Hebrew scripture, including the Pentateuch. The Jewish Bible is also referred to as the *Tanakh* or Holy Scriptures. The word *tanakh* is an acronym of the three parts of the Jewish Bible: Torah, the Five Books of Moses; Nevitim, the Prophets; and Kethuvim, the Writings.

Lastly, Torah is also the name of the physical scroll, comprised of the original writings of the early Hebrew scribes of the Pentateuch, traditionally found in synagogues around the world.

Tzaddik: A righteous person who not only behaves in a moral way, but also always goes out of his way to help other people who might be in some kind of trouble.

Zohar: The Hebrew name for The Book of Radiance, considered the primary text of the Kabbalah.

ACKNOWLEDGMENTS

This book simply would have been impossible without the help and guidance of writer and editor Susan Piperato, so I extend a very special thank you to her. I would also like to thank my publisher, Paul Cohen, who guided me throughout this process and was so patient each step of the way. If nothing else, by doing this project, I made a new friend!

Thank you to my congregants, who have been an inspiration for me on a daily basis regarding this book, especially Vera Kaplan, who gave me the idea to undertake this project, and Richard Chazen, Marty Rutberg, and Craig Snyder, who have been so supportive throughout the process. Thank you also to chef Richard Copedge from the Culinary Institute of America, who guided me on the baking recipes.

A special thank you goes to my mother for her guidance in editing the book.

And lastly, but definitely not least—*Acharon acharon chaviv*—thanks to my dear wife Tzivie for her support and encouragement each day and, more importantly, for allowing me to use our home as a test kitchen and for putting up with all the messes I've made in the process. And thank you to our children, for being such wonderful taste testers.

About the Author

 Rabbi Hanoch Hecht is the spiritual leader of the Rhinebeck Jewish Center and the director of both Chabad of Dutchess County and Camp Emunah, one of the largest girls' camps in New York State.

As a member of an extended family of notable rabbis in the United States and around the world, Rabbi Hecht is the son of Rabbi Shea Hecht, a well-known activist in the Lubavitcher community in Brooklyn, NY, and the grandson of the late Rabbi Jacob J. Hecht, who was the ambassador and translator for the famed Lubavitcher Rebbe.

A recipient of the Dutchess County Regional Chamber of Commerce's 40 Under 40 Shaker Awards, Rabbi Hecht has taught kosher cooking at the Culinary Institute of America and was the first rabbi to appear on Food Network's *Chopped*, competing with a priest, a nun-in-training, and a pastor. His recipes exploring kosher and modern Jewish cuisine have been featured in publications all over the globe. Rabbi Hecht lives with his wife Tzivie and their family in Rhinebeck, NY. This is his first book.